CONFORMED TO HIS IMAGE

CONFORMED TO HIS IMAGE

OSWALD CHAMBERS

LONDON
MARSHALL, MORGAN & SCOTT, LTD
EDINBURGH

LONDON
MARSHALL, MORGAN & SCOTT, LTD.
33 LUDGATE HILL, E.C:4

AUSTRALIA & NEW ZEALAND
317 COLLINS STREET
MELBOURNE

SOUTH AFRICA
P.O. BOX 1720, STURK'S BUILDINGS
CAPE TOWN

CANADA
EVANGELICAL PUBLISHERS
366 BAY STREET
TORONTO

First published 1950
Second Impression 1955

*Printed in Great Britain
by W. & J. Mackay & Co., Ltd., Chatham*

CONTENTS

Christian Thinking

I cannot soar into the heights you show,
  Nor dive into the deeps that you reveal ;
But it is much that high things are to know,
  That deep things are to feel.

JEAN INGELOW.

THE safe position in Christian thinking is to remember that there are deeper depths than we can fathom, higher heights than we can know ; it keeps us reverent, keeps us from hardening off into a confined, cabined experience of our own.

Thinking is not of first importance ; life is of first importance. Neither in natural nor in spiritual life do we begin by thinking. Christian thinking means thinking on the basis of things, not thinking in pious terms. With many the experience is right, the life of God is there, but there has been no thinking on the basis of things, and when things hit, there is confusion. If we are going to think along Christian lines and know where to place our individual experiences, it is time we exercised ourselves intellectually as well as spiritually.

REDEMPTION

The Gospel to me is simply irresistible. Being the man I am, being full of lust and pride and envy and malice and hatred and false good, and all accumulated exaggerated misery —to me the Gospel of the grace of God, and the Redemption of Christ, and the regeneration and sanctification of the Holy Ghost, that Gospel is to me simply irresistible, and I cannot understand why it is not equally irresistible to every mortal man born of woman.

PASCAL.

Redemption is the great outside fact of the Christian faith ; it has to do not only with a man's experience of salvation, but with the basis of his thinking. The revelation of Redemption means that Jesus Christ came here in order that by means of His Death on the Cross He might put the whole human race on a redemptive basis, so making it possible for every man to get back into perfect communion with God. " I have finished the work which Thou gavest Me to do." What was finished ? The redemption of the world. Men are not *going* to be redeemed ; they *are* redeemed. " It is finished." It was not the salvation of individual men and women like you and me that was finished : the whole human race was put on the basis of Redemption. Do I believe it ? Let me think of the worst man I know, the man for whom I have no affinity, the man who is a continual thorn in my flesh, who is as mean as can be ; can I imagine that man being presented " perfect in Christ Jesus " ? If I can, I have got the beginning of Christian thinking. It ought to be an easy thing for the Christian who thinks to conceive of any and every kind of man being presented " perfect in Christ Jesus," but how seldom we do think ! If I am an earnest evangelical preacher I may say to a man, " Oh yes, I believe God can save you," while in my heart of hearts I don't believe there is much hope for him. Our unbelief stands as the supreme barrier to Jesus Christ's work in men's souls. " And He did not many mighty works there because of their unbelief " (Matthew xiii, 58). But once let me get over my own slowness of heart to believe in Jesus Christ's power to save, and I become a real generator of His power to men. " Neither is there salvation in any other ; for there is none other Name under heaven given among men, whereby we must be saved "—the solitary, incommunicable place of Jesus in our salvation ! Are we banking in unshaken faith on the Redemption, or do we allow men's sins and wrongs to so obliterate Jesus Christ's power to save that we hinder His reaching them ? " He that *believeth* on Me," i.e., active belief based on the Redemption—" out of him shall flow rivers of living water." We have to be so faithful to God that through us may come the awakening of those who have not yet realised that they are redeemed.

We must distinguish between the revelation of Redemption and the experience of regeneration. We don't *experience* life ; we are alive. We don't *experience* Redemption ; we experience regeneration, that is, we experience the life of God coming into our human nature, and immediately the life of God comes in it produces a surface of consciousness, but Redemption means a great deal more than a man is conscious of. The Redemption is not only for mankind, it is for the universe, for the material earth ; everything that sin and the devil have touched and marred has been completely redeemed by Jesus Christ. There is a day coming when the Redemption will be actually manifested, when there will be " a new heaven and a new earth," with a new humanity upon it. If Redemption is confounded with regeneration, we get confused. In the majority of cases men have had an experience of regeneration, but they have not thought about what produced the experience, and when the great revelation fact of the Redemption is expounded there is misunderstanding. All that a man experiences is believing in Jesus, but that experience is the gateway into the awe and wonder of the knowledge of God. " And this is life eternal, that they should know Thee the only true God."

The Bible deals with the fundamental underlying things of human life, and one of these fundamental things is the presence of a disposition of sin in every man. Solidarity means oneness of interests, and the phrase, " the solidarity of the human race " indicates that there is an underlying connection running straight through human life ; on the religious side this connection is the heredity of sin, which was introduced into the world through one man, not by the devil—" Wherefore, as by one man sin entered into the world . . . for that all have sinned " (Romans v, 12), and when the Apostle Paul says, " Knowing this, that our old man was crucified with Him," he is referring to this heredity. Through the Redemption we have deliverance from the disposition of sin which is within us, and severance from the body of sin to which we are connected by our " old man " ; that is, we are absolutely and completely delivered from sin both in disposition and in domination. " Being then made free from sin. . . ." Unless the universality of sin is recognised we will never understand the need for the Redemption. What the Redemption deals with is the sin of the whole human race, not primarily with the sins of individuals, but something far more fundamental, viz., the heredity of sin. Pseudo-evangelism singles out the individual, it prostitutes the terrific meaning of the Redemption into an individual possession, the salvation of *my* soul.

The basis of Christian thinking is that God has redeemed the world from the possibility of condemnation on account of the heredity of sin. " God was in Christ, reconciling the world unto Himself, not imputing their trespasses unto them." The revelation is not that Jesus Christ was punished for our sins, but " He hath made Him to be sin for us, who knew no sin ; that we might be made the righteousness of God in Him." God nowhere holds a man responsible for having inherited the disposition of sin any more than he is held responsible for being born. We have nothing to do with our birth or with what we inherit, because we had no choice in either. A man will say, " If I am not held responsible for having a wrong disposition, what am I held responsible for ? " God holds a man responsible for not allowing Jesus Christ to deliver him from the wrong disposition when he sees that that is what He came to do. A man gets the seal of condemnation when he sees the light, and prefers darkness (see John iii, 19).

If you look upon Jesus Christ from the common-sense standpoint you will never discern who He is ; but if you look upon Him as God " manifested in the flesh " for the purpose of putting the whole human race back to where God designed it to be, you get the meaning of Redemption. The great marvellous revelation of Redemption is that it atones for everyone ; men are " condemned to salvation " through the Cross of Christ. Discipleship is another matter. There are things to be brought about in this world that can only be done through those of us who are prepared to fulfil the conditions of discipleship. On the basis of the Redemption I can, by committing myself to Jesus Christ and by receiving His Spirit as a gift, become a disciple in my actual life ; that is, I can exhibit in my mortal flesh " the life also of Jesus."

MAN

. . . *what is man, that Thou art mindful of him ?* PSALM viii, 4.

Man and Mankind

And God created man in His own image, in the image of God created He him, male and female created He them. GENESIS i, 27.

There is only one *Begotten* Son of God, one *created* son of God, and multitudes of *regenerated* sons of God through the Redemption. These three stand in different categories.

The Bible speaks of only two men—Adam and Jesus Christ. " Mankind " is the term applied to the whole race of men, the mass of human beings. God did not make *us* in His own image ; He made the Federal Head of the race in His image. " In the day that God created man, in the likeness of God made He him : male and female created He them, and blessed them, and called their name Adam " —" Man " R. V. marg. (Genesis v, 2.) Both man and woman are required for the completed creation of God. Jesus Christ is the last Adam in this sense, viz.: that He reveals the characteristics of El-Shaddai, the Father-Mother God, all vested in the unique manifestation of the Incarnation.

Man as He Was

And the Lord God formed man of the dust of the ground, and breathed into his nostrils the breath of life. GENESIS ii, 7.

Man as God created him is a revelation fact, not a fact we get at by our common-sense. We have never seen Man. God *created* the earth and " *formed* man of the dust of the ground," that is, God did not make man's body by a creative fiat, He deliberately builded it out of the dust of created matter according to a design in the Divine mind. Adam and Jesus Christ both came direct from the hand of God. We are not creations of God, we are pro-created through progenitors, the heredity of the human race is mixed ; that accounts for all the perplexities. " And the Lord God formed man of the dust of the ground "—there is nothing the matter with matter ; what has gone wrong is the infection of material things by sin, which is not material. Sin is not in matter and material things ; if it were, it would be untrue to say that Jesus Christ, who " was made in the likeness of men," was " without sin."

Genesis ii, 7 reveals that man's nature was a spiritual, sensuous nature—he was made of the dust of the ground, and God breathed into his nostrils the breath of life. These two things, dust and Divinity, make up man. It is impossible for us to conceive what Adam was like before the Fall ; his body must have been dazzling with light through his spiritual communion with God. When he took his rule over himself he not only lost his communion with God, lost the covering of glory and light inconceivable to us, he lost the dominion God intended him to have had—" Thou madest him to have dominion over the works of Thy hands " : (Psalm viii, 6). Men who are their own masters are masters of nothing else. A man may feel he ought to be master of the life in the sea and air and earth, but he can only be master on the line God designed he should, viz., that he recognised God's dominion over him. The only Being who ever walked this earth as God designed man should was Jesus Christ. He was easily Master of all created things because He maintained a steadfast obedience to the word and the will of His Father. " What manner of man is this, that even the winds and the sea obey Him ? " (Matthew viii, 27). Man's personal powers are apt to be looked at as a marvellous promise of what he is going to be ; the Bible looks at man as a ruin of what he was designed to be. There have come down in mankind remnants, broken remnants, of the first creation, they are evidence of the magnificent structure God made in the beginning, but not promises of what man is going to be.

Man as He Is

. . . *and were by nature the children of wrath.* EPHESIANS ii, 3.

The words "*ye are of your father the devil*," (JOHN viii, 44,) were not addressed by Jesus to men generally, but to persistent religious disbelievers in Himself.

"By nature the children of wrath." The love of God and the wrath of God are obverse sides of the same thing, like two sides of a coin. The wrath of God is as positive as His love. God cannot be in agreement with sin. When a man is severed from God the basis of his moral life is chaos and wrath, not because God is angry, like a Moloch, it is His constitution of things. The wrath of God abides all the time a man persists in the way that leads away from God; the second he turns, he is faced with His love. Wrath is the dark line in God's face, and is expressive of His hatred of sin. Civilization is the gloss over chaos and wrath, we are so sheltered that we are blinded to our need of God, and when calamity comes there is nothing to hold to. Over and over again in the history of the world man has made life into chaos. Men try to find their true life in everything but God, but they cannot, they find the "insistence of the Feet" behind them all the time.

> But with unhurrying chase,
> And unperturb-ed pace,
> Deliberate speed, majestic instancy,
> They beat—and a Voice beat
> More instant than the Feet—
> "All things betray thee, who betrayest Me."
>
> *The Hound of Heaven*, by FRANCIS THOMPSON.

Every love and justice and nobility in the world is loyal to Jesus Christ, and only loyal to me when I recognise Him as their Source. The Incarnation is the very heart of God manifested on the plane of chaos and wrath; what Jesus Christ went through in a Time-phase is indicated in such words as these, "My God, My God, why hast Thou forsaken Me?" Jesus Christ came right straight down into the very depths of wrath, He clothed Himself with the humanity of the race that had fallen and could not lift itself, and in His own Person He annihilated the wrath until there is "no condemnation," no touch of the wrath of God, on those who are "in Christ Jesus."

Man as He Will Be

. . . He also did predestinate to be conformed to the image of His Son. ROMANS viii, 29.

God's order is seen in the first and the last; the middle is the record of man's attempt to arrange things in his own way. Man is to be again in the image of God, not by evolution, but by Redemption. The meaning of Redemption is not simply the regeneration of individuals, but that the whole human race is rehabilitated, put back to where God designed it to be, consequently any member of the human race can have the heredity of the Son of God put into him, viz.: Holy Spirit, by right of what Jesus did on the Cross. The task which confronted Jesus Christ was that He had to bring man, who is a sinner, back to God, forgive him his sin, and make him as holy as He is Himself; and He did it single-handed. The revelation is that Jesus Christ, the last Adam, was "made to be sin," the thing which severed man from God, and that He put away sin by the sacrifice of Himself—"that we might become the righteousness of God in Him." He lifted the human race back, not to where it was in the first Adam, He lifted it back to where it never was, viz.: to where He is Himself. "And it doth not yet appear what we shall be: but we know that, when He shall appear, we shall be like Him; for we shall see Him as He is."

SIN

To-day the Bible revelation of sin as a positive thing has been revolted against, and sin is dealt with only as something which is ostensibly wrong ; the Bible view is that there is something profoundly wrong at the basis of things. Sin is a revelation fact, not a common-sense fact. No natural man is ever bothered about sin ; it is the saint, not the sinner, who knows what sin is. If you confound *sin* with *sins*, you belittle the Redemption, make it " much ado about nothing." It is nonsense to talk about the need of Redemption to enable a man to stop committing sins—his own will power enables him to do that, a decent education will prevent him from breaking out into sinful acts, but to deny that there is *an heredity of sin* running straight through the human race, aims a blasphemous blow at the Redemption. The only word that expresses the enormity of sin is " Calvary."

Guilt remains guilt ; you cannot bully God into any such blessing as turns guilt to merit, or penalty to rewards. IBSEN.

Ibsen saw sin, but not Calvary ; not the Son of God as Redeemer. If it cost God Calvary to deal with sin, we have no business to make light of it.

God created Adam innocent, that is, he was intended to develop, not from evil to good, but from the natural to the spiritual by obedience, it was to be a natural progress. Adam switched off from God's design, instead of maintaining his dependence on God he took his rule over himself, and thereby introduced sin into the world. Sin is not wrong doing, it is wrong *being*, deliberate and emphatic independence of God. " Wherefore, as by one man sin entered into the world . . . for that all have sinned " (Romans v, 12). It is not now a question of development, the problem is that an opposing force has come in which always says " I won't " and never can be made to say " I will." " I won't " is not imperfect " I will " ; it never develops into " I will," its very nature is " shan't " and " won't." Sin is mutiny against God's rule ; not vileness of conduct, but red-handed anarchy. When you get sin revealed in you, you know that that phrase is not too strong. It is not that men are conscious anarchists—the devil is the only being in whom sin is conscious anarchy—but that a man perceives that that is the nature of sin once the light of God is thrown upon it ; it is " enmity against God," not " at enmity," it *is* enmity. This opposing principle is abnormal, it was not in human nature as God designed it. The exposition of the nature of sin rarely enters into my human consciousness, when it does I know there is nothing in my spirit to deliver me from it, I am powerless ; " sold under sin," said Paul. " Whosoever committeth sin is the servant of sin."

Bear in mind that it requires the Holy Ghost to convict a man of sin ; any man knows that immorality is wrong, his conscience tells him it is ; but it takes the Holy Ghost to convince a man that the thing he most highly esteems, viz. : is own self-government, is " an abomination in the sight of God." There is nothing more highly esteemed among men that self-realisation, but it is the one thing of which Jesus Christ is the enemy because its central citadel is independence of God. If a man can stand on his own feet morally—and many a man can—what does he want with Jesus Christ and His salvation ? with forgiveness ? Some men are driven to God by appalling conviction of sins, but conviction of sins is not conviction of *sin*. Conviction of sin never comes as an elementary experience. If you try to convict a man of sin to begin with you draw him to a plan of salvation, but not to Jesus Christ.

B

The essence of sin is my claim to my right to myself, it goes deeper down than all the sins that ever were committed. Sin can't be forgiven because it is not an act ; you can only be forgiven for the sins you commit, not for an heredity. " If we confess our sins, He is faithful and just to forgive us our sins " : *sin* must be cleansed by the miracle of God's grace. It does not awaken antipathy in a man when you tell him God will forgive him his sins because of what Jesus did on the Cross, but it does awaken antipathy when you tell him he has to give up his right to himself. Nothing is so much resented as the idea that I am not to be my own master. " If any man will be My disciple," said Jesus, " let him deny himself," i.e., deny his right to himself, not give up external sins, those are excrescences. The point is, am I prepared deliberately to give up my right to myself to Jesus Christ ? prepared to say, " Yes, take complete control " ? If I am, Jesus Christ has gained a disciple. We don't go in for making disciples to-day, it takes too long ; we are all for passionate evangelism—taken up with adding to the statistics of " saved souls," adding to denominational membership, taken up with the things which show splendid success. Jesus Christ took the long, long trail—" If any man will be My disciple, let him deny himself "—" Take time to make up your mind." Men were not to be swept into the Kingdom on tidal waves of evangelism, not to have their wits paralysed by supernatural means ; they were to come deliberately, knowing what they were doing. One life straight through to God on the ground of discipleship is more satisfactory in His sight than numbers who are saved but go no further. Over and over again men and women who should stand in the forefront for God are knocked clean out when a crisis comes, the reason is not external wrong-doing, but something has never been given up, there is something in which Jesus Christ has not had His right of way, and the discipleship is marred. God will give us ample opportunity of proving whether we have ever really given up the right to ourselves to Jesus Christ. The one who has offers no hindrance to the working of the Holy Spirit through him.

NEW BIRTH

As soon as we begin to examine the foundations of our salvation we are up against the thoughts of God, and as Christians we ought to be busy thinking God's thoughts after Him. That is where we fall short ; we are delighted with the fact that " once I was this, and now I am that," but simply to have a vivid experience is not sufficient if we are to be at our best for God. It is because of the refusal to think on Christian lines that Satan has come in as angel of light and switched off numbers of God's children in their head, with the result that there is a divorce between heart and head. There is nothing simpler under heaven than to become a Christian, but after that it is not easy ; we have to " leave the word of the beginning of Christ and press on unto full growth." (Hebrews vi, 1, R.V. marg.)

Except a man be born again, he cannot see the kingdom of God. JOHN iii, 3.

There is no natural law whereby a man can be born a second time—Nicodemus was right there : *How can a man be born when he is old ?* No man ought to need to be born again ; the fact that he does indicates that something has gone wrong with the human race. According to modern thinking, man is a great being in the making ; his attainments are looked on as a wonderful promise of what he is going to be ; we are obsessed with the evolutionary idea. Jesus Christ talks about a revolution—" Ye must be born again." The evolutionary idea doesn't cover all the facts. Not every man needs to be converted ; conversion simply means turning in another direction, it may be a right or a wrong direction; but every man needs to be born from above if he is going to see the kingdom of God. In listening to some presentations of the Gospel you get the impression that a man has to be a blackguard before Jesus Christ can do anything for him. It is true that Jesus Christ can make a saint out of any material, but the man down-and-out in sin is not the only class He deals with. It was to Nicodemus, a godly upright man, not to a sinner as we understand the term, that He said, " Marvel not that I said unto thee, Ye must be born again." " Class yourself with the whole human race, it is necessary for you, the Teacher of Israel, to be born again." It is easier to think about the sensational cases of men being transformed and lifted into a new realm by God's grace, but there are hundreds of men who are not sinners in the external sense. Does Jesus Christ do anything for them?

Many Christians don't seem to know what happened to them when they were born again, that is why they continually go back to the initial experience of having had their sins forgiven, they don't " press on unto full growth." In the New Testament new birth is always spoken of in terms of sanctification, not of salvation; to be saved means that a man receives the gift of eternal life, which is " the gift of God "; sanctification means that his spirit becomes the birthplace of the Son of God. " My little children, of whom I am again in travail until Christ be formed in you." (Galatians iv, 19.) If Jesus Christ is going to be in me, He must come into me from the outside; He must be " formed " in me. It is not a question of being saved from hell, the Redemption has to do with that; this is the Redemption at work in my conscious life. I become a " Bethlehem " for the life of the Son of God. The part of human nature is to sacrifice itself to nourish that life, and every now and again there are things demanded by the life of the Son of God in me that my human nature neither likes nor understands. What Simeon said to Mary—" A sword shall pierce through thine own soul "—is true of my human nature. Am I willing for my human nature to be sacrificed in order that the life of the Son of God in me may be nourished, or do I only want Him to see me through certain difficulties ? The way the life of the Son of God is nourished in me is by prayer and Bible revelation, and by obedience when a crisis comes.

When I am born again my human nature is not different, it is the same as before, I am related to life in the same way, I have the same bodily organs, but the mainspring is different, and I have to see now that all my members are dominated by the new disposition (see Romans vi, 13, 19). There is only one kind of human nature, and that is the human nature we have all got ; and there is only one kind of holiness, the holiness of Jesus Christ. Give Him " elbow-room," and He will manifest Himself in you, and other people will recognise Him. Human beings know human beings too well to mistake where goodness comes from ; when they see certain characteristics they will know they come only from the indwelling of Jesus. It is not the manifestation of noble human traits, but of a real family likeness to Jesus. It is *His* gentleness, *His* patience, *His* purity, never mine. The whole art of spirituality is that my human nature should retire and let the new disposition have its way. We are told to " follow His steps," but we can't do it ; the heredity in us is not the same as it is in Jesus. Anyone who reads the Sermon on the Mount with his eyes open knows that something must happen if it is going to be lived out in him, for he has not the goods on board to produce the result. There is only one Being who can live the Sermon on the Mount and that is the Son of God. If I

will walk in the light as God is in the light, then the holy
nature of Jesus manifests itself in me. It is not that I
receive an impartation of the Divine nature and then am
left to work it out by myself—" Jesus Christ is made unto
us sanctification," that is, *He* is the holy nature which we
receive.

" Blessed are the poor in spirit," said Jesus, because it is
through that poverty I enter His Kingdom ; I cannot
enter it as a good man or woman, I can only enter it as a
complete pauper. The knowledge of my poverty brings me
to the frontier where Jesus Christ works, as long as a man is
sufficient for himself, God can do nothing for him. A man
may be " pagan-ly " all right, in fact a pagan is a delightful
man to know, he is not " out at elbows," not troubled or
upset, and he cannot understand why you should talk of
the need to be born again. The born-again man has been
put on the basis of a new construction of humanity, consequently for a time he is chaotic, disturbed, broken, and
at this stage he is not so desirable as the man who represents
the climax of the natural life. Our natural virtues are our
deepest inheritance, but when the miracle of new birth is
experienced, the first thing that happens is the corruption
of those virtues because they can never come anywhere
near what God demands. Jesus Christ loved moral beauty,
(see Mark x, 21), but He never said it would do. The
natural virtues are a delight to God because He designed
them, they are fine and noble, but behind them is a disposition which may cause a man's morality to go by the board.
What Jesus Christ does in new birth is to put in a disposition
that transforms morality into holiness. He came to put
into the man who knows he needs it His own heredity of
holiness ; to bring him into a oneness with God which he
never had through natural birth. " That they may be one,
even as We are one."

The experimental aspect of Redemption is repentance; the only proof that a man is born from above is that he brings forth " fruits meet for repentance." That is the one characteristic of New Testament regeneration, and it hits desperately hard because the Holy Spirit brings conviction on the most humiliating lines. Many a powerless, fruitless Christian life is the result of a refusal to obey in some insignificant thing—"first go." It is extraordinary what we are brought up against when the Holy Spirit is at work in us, and the thing that fights longest against His demands is my prideful claim to my right to myself. The only sign of regeneration in practical experience is that we begin to make our life in accordance with the demands of God. Jesus Christ did not only come to present what God's normal man should be, He came to make the way for everyone of us to get there, and the gateway is His Cross. I cannot begin by imitating Jesus Christ, but only by being born into His Kingdom; then when I have been regenerated and have received the heredity of the Son of God, I find that His teaching belongs to that heredity, not to my human nature.

All this means great deliberation on our part. God does not expect us to understand these things in order to be saved, salvation is of God's free grace; but He does expect us to do our bit in appreciation of His " so great salvation."

REPENTANCE

Never mistake remorse for repentance; remorse simply puts a man in hell while he is on earth, it carries no remedial quality with it at all, nothing that betters a man. An un-awakened sinner knows no remorse, but immediately a man recognizes his sin he experiences the pain of being gnawed by a sense of guilt, for which punishment would be a heaven of relief, but no punishment can touch it. In the case of Cain (see Genesis iv, 9–14) remorse is seen at its height : " Mine iniquity is greater than can be forgiven." (iv, 13, R.V. marg.) Cain was in the condition of being found out by his own sin ; his conscience recognized what he had done, and he knew that God recognized it too. Remorse is not the recognition that I am detected by somebody else, I can defy that ; remorse comes when intellectually and morally, I recognize my own guilt. It is a desperate thing for me to realize that I am a sneak, that I am sensual and proud, that is my sin finding *me* out. The Holy Spirit never convicts of sin until He has got Jesus Christ pretty close up ; a human being would like to convict of sin before Jesus Christ is there. The classic experience of Cain has all lesser experiences folded up in it ; few of us are actually murderers, but we are all criminals in potentiality —" Whosoever hateth his brother is a murderer " (1 John iii, 15) ; and one of the greatest humiliations in work for God is that we are never free from the reminder by the Holy Spirit of what we might be in actuality but for the grace of God.

When any sin is recalled with a gnawing sense of guilt, this " biting again " of remorse, watch carefully that it does not make you whine and indulge in sulks about the consequences. The beginning of sulks is the blaming of everybody but yourself, and every step you take in that direction leads further away from God and from the possibility of repentance. Whenever the lash of remorse comes, never try to prevent it, every bit of it is deserved. And if you are a worker, never tell a lie out of sympathy and say, " Oh well, you don't need to feel like that, you couldn't help it." Never tell a lie to another soul. The temptation is tremendously strong to sympathise with a man and prove a traitor to his soul's true instincts ; he may fling off from you at a tangent, but truth will tell in the end.

Reformation, which means to form again or renew, is a law that works in human nature apart from the grace of God as well as after regeneration ; if it takes place apart from regeneration it is simply the reformation of a rebel. Certain forms of wild oats bring forth their crop and pass and a man becomes different in conduct, but he is a deeply entrenched unregenerate person. That a man stops being bad and becomes good may have nothing to do with salvation ; the only one sign that a man is saved is repentance. Instances of reformation apart from the grace of God can be multiplied because there is something in human nature that reacts towards reformation when once the right influence is brought to bear at the right time, e.g., the boy who won't reform for his father's threats or his schoolmaster's punishment, will experience a reaction towards reformations through his mother's love. Again, though a bad man will become worse in the presence of suspicious people, when with little children he experiences a reaction towards reformation. If being in the presence of a good man or woman does not produce a reaction towards goodness in me, I am in a bad way. The Apostle Paul sums up this law when he says, " . . . not knowing that the goodness of God leadeth thee to repentance ? " (Romans ii, 4.)

" And Zacchæus stood, and said unto the Lord, Behold, Lord, the half of my goods I give to the poor ; and if I have taken anything from any man by false accusation, I restore him fourfold." (Luke xix, 8.) Why did Zacchæus say that ? who had said a word about his peculations ! The desire to make restitution was stirred through his coming into the presence of Jesus, and was a sign of the working of this inevitable law of reaction. Restitution means the determination to do right to everybody I have " done."

and it is astonishing the things the Holy Spirit will remind us of that we have to put right. Over and over again during times of revival and great religious awakening workers are presented with this puzzle, that people do unquestionably make restitution—men who stole pay up like sheep, with no notion why they do it, and if the worker is not well taught he will mistake this for the work of the Holy Spirit and a sign that they are born again, when the fact is that the truth has been so clearly put that it caused their nature to react towards reformation. The thing to do with people in that condition is to get them to *receive* something from God.

Luke xi, 25 is a picture of clear, sweeping reformation, the house " swept and garnished " ; but what our Lord points out is the peril of a moral victory unused because the heart is left empty. The man who reforms without any knowledge of the grace of God is the subtlest infidel with regard to the need of regeneration. It is a good thing to have the heart swept, but it becomes the worst thing if the heart is left vacant for spirits more evil than itself to enter ; Jesus said that " the last state of that man becometh worse than the first." Reformation is a good thing, but like every other good thing it is the enemy of the best. Regeneration means filling the heart with something positive, viz., the Holy Spirit.

Repentance is the experimental side of Redemption and is altogether different from remorse or reformation. " Repentance " is a New Testament word and cannot be applied outside the New Testament. We all experience remorse, disgust with ourselves over the wrong we have done when we are found out by it, but the rarest miracle of God's grace is the sorrow that puts an end for ever to the thing for which I am sorry. Repentance involves the receiving of a totally new disposition so that I never do the wrong thing again. The marvel of conviction of sin, of forgiveness, and of the holiness of God are so interwoven that the only for-given man is the holy man. If God in forgiving me does not turn me into the standard of the Forgiver, to talk about being saved from hell and made right for heaven is a juggling trick to get rid of the responsibility of seeing that my life justifies God in forgiving me. The great element in practical Christianity—and that is the only kind of Christianity there is—is this note of repentance, which means I am willing to go all lengths so long as God's law which I have broken is cleared in my case—" . . . that Thou mayest be justified when Thou speakest, and be clear when Thou judgest." (Psalm li, 4.) Have I ever had a moment before God when I have said, " My God, I deserve all that Thou canst bring on me as punishment for breaking Thy holy law—' against Thee, Thee only, have I sinned, and done that which is evil in Thy sight '"? The essence of repent-ance is that it destroys the lust of self-vindication; wherever that lust resides the repentance is not true. Repentance brings us to the place where we are willing to receive any punishment under heaven so long as the law we have broken is justified. That is repentance, and I think I am right in saying that very few of us know anything at all about it. We have the idea nowadays that God is so loving and gentle and kind that all we need do is to say we feel sorry for the wrong we have done and we will try to be better. That is not repentance; Repentance means that I am re-made on a plane which justifies God in forgiving me.

Once get this kind of thinking into your mind and you will understand what is meant by conviction of sin. The repentant man experiences the humiliating conviction that he has broken the law of God and he is willing to accept, on God's terms, the gift of a new life which will prove sufficient in him to enable him to live a holy life, not here-after, but here and now. Strictly speaking, repentance is a

gift of God ; a man cannot repent when he chooses. Repentance does not spring out of the human heart, it springs
from a ground outside the human heart, viz., the ground
of the Redemption.

REALITY

1. *The Will to Believe the Redeemer.*

. . . *blessed are they that have not seen, and yet have
believed.* JOHN xx, 29. cf. JOHN xi, 40.

Reality is the thing which works out absolutely solidly
true in my personal life, but I must be careful not to confound the reality of my experience with Reality itself. For
instance, when I am born again I am not conscious of the
Redemption of my Lord, the one thing that is real to me is
that I have been born again ; but if I watch the working
of the Holy Spirit I find that He takes me clean out of
myself till I no longer pay any attention to my experiences,
I am concerned only with the Reality which produced those
experiences, viz., the Redemption. If I am left with my
experiences, they have not been produced by the Redemption. If experience is made the only guide it will produce
that peculiar type of isolated life that is never found in the
New Testament.

We say " seeing is believing," but it is not ; we must
believe a thing is possible before we would believe it even
though we saw it. Belief must be the will to believe, and I
can never will to believe without a violent effort on my part
to dissociate myself from all my old ways of looking at
things and putting myself right over on to God. It is God
who draws me, my relationship is to Him, consequently the
issue of will comes in at once—Will I transact on what God
says ? Never discuss with anyone when God speaks ; dis-
cussion on spiritual matters is impertinent. God never

discusses with anyone. Let me stake my all, blindly, as far as feelings are concerned, on the Reality of the Redemption, and before long that Reality will begin to tell in my actual life, which will be the evidence that the transaction has taken place. But there must be the deliberate surrender of will, not a surrender to the persuasive power of a personality, but a deliberate launching forth on God and what He says. Remember, you must urge the will to an issue ; you must come to the point where you *will* to believe the Redeemer, and deliberately wash your hands of the consequences.

In testing for ourselves our relation to Reality we are not left in a vague fog, we have the Word of God expressing God to us, and the Word of God, our Lord Jesus Christ, expresses Himself to us through His teaching, made vitally applicable to every domain of our human life. Any attempt to divorce the words of God from the Word of God leads to unreality ; the words of God are only vitally real when we are in a right relationship to God through the Word. Men worship an intellectual creed, and you can't dispute it because it is logically correct, but it does not produce saints ; it produces stalwarts and stoics but not New Testament saints, because it is based on adherence to the literal words rather than on a vital relationship to God, who is the one abiding Reality. In the final issue Christian principles are found to be antichrist, i.e., an authority other than Christ Himself. It is quite possible to have an intellectual appreciation of the Redemption without any experience of supernatural grace ; an experience of supernatural grace comes by committing myself to a Person, not to a creed or a conviction. I can never find Reality by looking within ; the only way I can get at Reality is by dumping myself outside myself on to Someone else, viz.: God, immediately I do I am brought in touch with Reality.

2. *The Will to Receive the Redeemer.*

But as many as received Him . . . JOHN i, 12–13.

We do not create truth, we receive it. There are things which you perceive clearly, but are they real to you ? They are not real if you have never been through a transaction of will in connection with them, your perception is based on the weaving of your own brain, not on the knowledge of Someone who knows you. The Giver is God, and every gift He offers is based on His knowledge of us ; our attitude is to be that of receiving from Him all the time, and in this way we become sons and daughters of God. It requires the greatest effort, and produces the greatest humility, to receive anything from God, we would much sooner earn it. Receiving is the evidence of a disciple of the Lord ; reasoning about it is the indication of a dictator to God. Effective repentance is witnessed to by my receiving from God instead of reasoning why God should give it to me. When I am willing to be such a fool as to accept, that is repentance ; the other is rational pride. We can only get at Reality by means of our conscience which ultimately embraces both head and heart. There is always a practical proof when we do get at Reality, viz., actuality is made in accord with it. Does your intellect make you in accord actually with what you think ? Of course it does not. Read the lives of some of the most intellectual men, men whose æsthetic sensibilities are of the finest order, but their actual life won't bear looking at. I cannot get at Reality by my intellect or by emotion, but only by my conscience bringing me in touch with the Redemption. When the Holy Spirit gets hold of my conscience He convicts me of unreality, and when I respond to God I come in touch with Reality and experience a sense of wonder—" That He should have done this for me ! " It is not extravagant, it is the result of a totally new adjustment, a relation to the Reality which has been created in me by means of my abandonment to Jesus Christ.

3. *The Will to Obey the Redeemer.*

If ye love Me, keep My commandments. JOHN xiv, 15, 21, 23 ; xv, 10–12.

These verses are specimens of many that reveal what is to be the abiding attitude of the saint, viz.: obeying the commandments of One whom we can only believe by will, and whose gifts we can only receive by will. We will to believe Him, then we obey by will. These exercises of the will are essential to the wholesome upkeep of a saint's actual life. The effort on the human side is to maintain the childlike relation to God, receiving from Him all the time, then obedience works out in every detail. When a man is rightly related to God it is the Holy Ghost who works through him, and as long as he maintains the will to believe, the will to receive and the will to obey, the life of Jesus is manifested in his mortal flesh.

Beware of any hesitation to abandon to God. It is the meanest characteristics of our personality that are at work whenever we hesitate, there is some element of self-interest that won't submit to God. When we do cut the shore lines and launch forth, what happens is a great deal more than a vision of the indwelling of God ; what happens is the positive miracle of the Redemption at work in us, and we have patiently to make it permeate everything. Our relationship to God is first that of personality, not of intellect ; intellect comes in after to explain what has transpired, and it is the ordering of the mind that makes a man a teacher and an instructor. Be stably rooted in God and then begin to know, begin to use those rusty brains.

Beware of having an overweening interest in your own
character so that you are inclined to believe in God on that
account ; at the same time be careful to allow nothing that
would hinder your relationship to God, because any im-
pairing of that relationship hinders Him in getting at other
souls through you. Continually revise your relationship to
God until the only certainty you have is not that you are
faithful, but that He is. Priggishness is based on concern
for my own whiteness, a pathetic whine—" I am afraid I
am not faithful " : " I am afraid I shall never be what God
wants me to be." Get into contact with Reality and what
you feel no longer matters to you, the one terrific Reality
is God.

An abiding way of maintaining our relation to Reality is
intercession. Intercession means that I strive earnestly to
have my human soul moved by the attitude of my Lord to
the particular person I am praying for. That is where our
work lies, and we shirk it by becoming active workers ;
we do the things that can be tabulated and scheduled, and
we won't do the one thing that has no snares. Intercession
keeps the relationship to God completely open. You cannot
intercede if you do not believe in the Reality of Redemption,
you will turn intercession into futile sympathy with human
beings which only increases their submissive content to
being out of touch with God. Intercession means getting
the mind of Christ about the one for whom we pray, that
is what is meant by " filling up that which is behind of the
afflictions of Christ " ; and that is why there are so few
intercessors. Be careful not to enmesh yourself in more
difficulties than God has engineered for you to know ; if you
know too much, more than God has engineered, you cannot
pray, the condition of the people is so crushing that you
can't get through to Reality. The true intercessor is the one
who realises Paul's meaning when he says, " for we know

not what we should pray for as we ought : but the Spirit Himself maketh intercession for us with groanings which cannot be uttered." (Romans viii, 26.)

THE HOLY SPIRIT

1. *The Holy Spirit and Revelation Purpose.*

. . . *holy men of God spake as they were moved by the Holy Ghost.* 2 PETER i, 21.

Bear in mind that there is a two-fold attitude to be maintained in dealing with the Self-revelation of God—first, its historic setting ; second, its value to me personally. It is essential to have an historic basis for our Christian faith : our faith must be centred in the Life and Death of the historic Jesus. Why is it that that Life and Death have an importance out of all proportion to every other historic fact ? Because there the Redemption is brought to a focus. Jesus Christ was not a Man who twenty centuries ago lived on this earth for thirty-three years and was crucified ; He was God Incarnate, manifested at one point of history. All before looked forward to that point ; all since look back to it. The presentation of this fact produces what no other fact in the whole of history ever could produce, viz. : the miracle of God at work in human souls. The death of Jesus was not the death of a martyr, it was the revelation of the Eternal heart of God. That is why the Cross is God's last word ; that does not mean God is not speaking still, it means that He is saying nothing contrary to the Cross.

The tendency abroad to-day is to do away with the historic setting of the revelation of God in Christ in the Gospels, to do away with what the apostles wrote, and say, " All that is needed is to receive the Holy Spirit and we will have a ' private interpretation ' of our own." But

C

" no prophecy of the scripture is of any private interpretation. For the prophecy came not in old time by the will of man : but holy men spake as they were moved by the Holy Ghost ". That makes it incumbent upon us to be reverent to a degree with what the apostles wrote. The Epistles are not the cogitations of men of extraordinary spiritual genius, but the posthumous work of the Ascended Christ and they have therefore a peculiar significance in the programme of Redemption. The Holy Ghost used these men, with all their personal idiosyncrasies, to convey God's message of salvation to the world. Our Lord, so to speak, incarnated Himself in them—the message of God must always be incarnated, but it remains the message *of God*. The Epistles are the exposition of why God became " manifest in the flesh," and when by submissive reception I commit myself to that revelation, the Holy Ghost begins to interpret to me what Jesus Christ did on the Cross.

" Neither pray I for these alone, but for them which shall believe on Me through their word " (John xvii, 20). Everyone who believes on Jesus, believes on Him " through their word." In the experience of salvation all are alike ; in the matter of authoritative inspiration the apostles stand alone ; their word is as final as Jesus Christ's. We have no counterpart to that. The inspiration the Holy Ghost gives us is not for revelation purposes, but for insight into the revelation already given. Apostolic inspiration is not an experience, it is as great a miracle as the Incarnation. The one great need is for the Holy Spirit to be received, because He will open up to us not only our own salvation, and the whole of the New Testament revelation, He will open up the treasures of the Old Testament—" even the mystery which hath been hid from ages and from generations, but now is made manifest to His saints . . . which is *Christ in you*, the hope of glory " (Colossians i, 26–27).

2. *The Holy Spirit and Redemptive Preaching.*

For the preaching of the cross is to them that perish foolishness. . . It pleased God by the foolishness of preaching to save them that believe. 1 CORINTHIANS i, 18, 21.

We are nowhere told to preach salvation, or sanctification, or Divine healing ; we are told to lift up Jesus, who is the Redeemer, and He will produce His redemptive results in the souls of men. If I preach only the effects of the Redemption, describe in persuasive speech what God has done for me, nothing will happen. It is only when I am humble enough, and stupid enough, to preach the Cross that the miracle of God takes place. The " preaching of the Cross " creates that which enables a man to believe in God, because the Cross *is* the manifestation of the Redemption. The Cross " condemns men to salvation." The " foolishness of preaching " is the way God has chosen to make the Redemption efficacious in human lives. You can't *persuade* a man to believe in God ; belief in God is not an act of the intellect, it is a moral creation produced by the interaction of God's Spirit and my spirit in willing obedience ; intellect comes in afterwards to explain what has happened. In preaching the Cross we use our intellect, not to prove that Jesus died, but to present the fact of His death. The danger is to give expression to subjective experiences we have had ; but that will never produce the same experiences in others, it is personal testimony and has its right place, but it is not " preaching the Cross." The bedrock permanent thing in Christian experience is not the accidental bits of God's particular manifestation of it in you and me, the bedrock permanent thing is the Redemption, and our particular experiences of it, slight or profound, are simply meant to introduce us to that Reality.

3. *The Holy Spirit and Revealing Power.*

Howbeit when He, the Spirit of truth, is come, He will guide you into all truth . . . He shall glorify Me. JOHN xvi, 13–14.

If an expositor has never realised the need to receive, recognise and rely on the Holy Spirit, he takes little account of the Cross but says, " Let us come to the teachings of Jesus." Our Lord never placed the emphasis on what He taught, neither do the apostles ; they place all the emphasis on the Cross. Why ? Because they were shrewd and intelligent ? No, because the Holy Ghost inspired them to put the emphasis there. " But God forbid that I should glory , save in the Cross of our Lord Jesus Christ." Our Lord is not the great Teacher of the world, He is the Saviour of the world and the Teacher of those who believe in Him, which is a radically different matter. His teaching is of no use saving to agonise mankind with its unattainable ideals until men are made anew through the Cross. Unless I am born from above the only result of the teachings of Jesus is to produce despair. People say that Jesus Christ came to teach us to be good ; He never did ! All the teaching in the world about a man having a pure heart won't make it pure. Our Lord's teaching has no power in it unless I possess His nature. When I am born from above it is the conscientious relationship between my individual life and Jesus Christ that keeps my conduct right. Once I am brought into contact with Reality I begin to experience the power of the Redemption as it applies to every phase of life.

For He shall receive of Mine, and shall shew it unto you. JOHN xvi, 14.

The spirit of antichrist is that spirit which " dissolves by analysis " the Person of Jesus—" someone unique, but not what the New Testament claims." To preach the Jesus of the Gospels at the expense of the Christ of the Epistles is a false thing, such a false thing that it is antichrist to the very core, because it is a blow direct at what Jesus said the Holy Spirit would do, viz.: expound Him to the disciples, and " through their word " to innumerable lives to the end of Time. If I say " Of course God would never convey a right interpretation of Himself through a handful of men like the disciples," I am casting a slur on what Jesus said, telling Him that His reliance on God's promise of the Spirit was without justification ; that His basis of confidence on the Holy Spirit's revelation of Himself to the disciples was misplaced. When our Lord told the disciples they would do " greater works," His reliance was not on them, but on the gift of the Spirit which He was to receive from the Father and shed forth on them. Everything Jesus said the Holy Spirit would do, He has done, and the New Testament is the revelation of it.

4. *The Holy Spirit and Revealed Proclamation.*

He gave some, apostles . . . for the edifying of the body of Christ. EPHESIANS iv, 11, 12.

Our Lord gave the disciples the gift of the Holy Spirit as their equipment for proclaiming the Gospel to the world ; in the same way the Holy Spirit comes into my personal life to bring me out of my individual narrowness into the universal purpose of God. When I want to translate all God's redemptive work into the consciousness of being saved, I become a pious humbug. God does not save me in order that I may feel saved, but to take me up into His redemptive purpose. Christian experience must be expounded as it emerges in its most extraordinary and tragic form, not in order to make that form the standard, but as giving the basis to which every experience is to be traced. You say, " I have never had such profound conviction of sin, such depth of repentance, as the apostle Paul, therefore I can't be a true Christian." We are not meant to imitate Paul in his experience, but to remember that that profound experience gives us the right direction for tracing where our own experience comes from. Paul never says, " Follow my way of getting into Christ," because no two people ever come the same way *into* Christ, yet they must follow the same ways *in* Christ. Experience is simply the doorway into Reality, if I stick in the doorway I get cold and die, die away from Reality; I must go through the doorway, and in the classic experiences we get the door widest open.

" For the edifying of the body of Christ." The New Testament is the product of the Holy Ghost, we are literally fed into the Body of Christ by its words. " Feed My sheep," said Jesus, and all down the ages the words of the New Testament have fed the children of God; if we try to nourish ourselves in any other way we produce abortions, what the writer to the Hebrews calls " bastards." The point for me is not simply that I appreciate with my mind what the New Testament declares, but that I am brought into such a relationship with God that His words become serviceable through me to others. It sounds pathetic to talk about " drawing on the life of Jesus " to keep the needs of my physical life supplied; but that is not His meaning; it is drawing on the life of Jesus through His Word that He might serve out nourishment to others through me.

NATURAL AND PERSONAL LIFE

Never run away with the idea that you are a person who has a spirit, has a soul, and has a body; you are a person that *is* spirit, soul and body. Man is one; body, soul and spirit are terms of definition. My body is the manifest "me." Some of us are so dominated by the body that our spirit lives only in the physical domain, instead of the physical being slowly taken into the spiritual by a series of moral choices. Our spirit goes no further than we bring our body. One of the best means of spiritual progress is to learn to deny the body in a great number of unnecessary ways. (cf. 1 Corinthians ix, 27.)

1 Corinthians xv, 46 (" Howbeit that was not first which is spiritual, but that which is natural ; and afterward that which is spiritual ") lays down the fundamental basis of the way God deals with man all through—first the natural, then the spiritual. The whole purpose of a human personality is to turn the natural life into a spiritual life by sacrifice. The Bible never speaks of the natural life as sinful, it contrasts it with the spiritual, e.g., " the natural man receiveth not the things of the Spirit of God . . . neither can he know them because they are spiritually discerned. But he that is spiritual discerneth all things " (1 Corinthians ii, 14–15).

Adam, the Federal Head of the human race, was designed by God to take part in his own development, that is, he was intended to turn the natural into the spiritual by a series of choices, which would mean moral progress. The natural life is the " lamb " for sacrifice. It is not fanaticism, but the sacrificing of what is absolutely legitimate and right and making it spiritual by obedience. That is the only way personality is exhibited in its true form. It has nothing to do with sin ; there would have been sacrifice whether there had been sin or not because of God's design of man. It was not a sin for our Lord to have a human body, it was not a sin for Him to eat, but it would have been sin for Him to eat during the forty days in the wilderness because His Father's will was otherwise. Our Lord stands as the presentation of God's normal Man, and when by regeneration His life is formed in us we have to transform the natural life into a spiritual life by obedience to the will of God, letting Him engineer our circumstances as He will. We are not fundamentally free, external circumstances are not in our hands, they are in God's hands, the one thing in which we are free is in our personal relationship to God. We are not responsible for the circumstances we are in, but we are responsible for the way we allow those circumstances to affect us ; we can either allow them to get on top of us, or we can allow them to transform us into what God wants us to be. If we go under in circumstances we are held responsible because God has promised an absolutely overcoming Spirit to any man who will receive Him. If you are at a loss to know how to get at what God wants you to be, listen to the Lord Jesus. He says, " If you ask God He will plant in you the very Spirit that is in Me " (see Luke xi, 13). If you receive the Holy Spirit you find that circumstances will never have power to do anything but give you the chance of sacrificing the natural to the spiritual and proving you are a son or daughter of God.

" And the Lord God . . . breathed into his nostrils the breath of life " (Genesis ii, 7), i.e., God breathed into man that which became man's spirit, that is the indestructible factor in every human being. Man is, and he will never be un-created. Man has kinship with God as no other creation of God has ; his true kinship is with God and nowhere else. When I receive the Holy Spirit He lifts my personality back into its primal relationship with God. Holy Spirit coming into my spirit never becomes my spirit ; He energizes my spirit and enables me " to will and to do of His good pleasure."

God has put man in an experimental sphere and if he

refuses to turn the natural into the spiritual he will find himself dominated by the body, it will chain him down and make him a slave. The personality of a man apart from the Spirit of God becomes enslaved to the desires of the flesh. The marvel of the life of God in a man is that he never need be dominated by anything other than spirit— " Walk in the Spirit, and ye shall not fulfil the lust of the flesh." (Galatians v, 17.) But if you don't sacrifice your natural inclinations and impulses to the will and the word of God, you are likely to be tripped up by any of the things Paul mentions : " Now the works of the flesh are manifest, which are these . . ." It will test a man to the limit to take his stand on the Redemption and the indwelling of the Holy Spirit and prove in actual life what God has put in him by regeneration. We are taken up with the "soul-saving" line instead of the line of character-building on the basis of the Redemption, consequently you get people who are gloriously saved but they have never gone on to sacrifice the natural to the spiritual—never put the knife to the throat of an appetite, never recognised pig-headed obstinacy, never got on the track of that green-eyed monster, envy. " But those things can't be in me now that I am saved "—and they are painted in glaring colours ! When the Holy Spirit begins to unearth the works of the flesh in you, don't temporize, don't whitewash them ; don't call suspicion, discernment of the spirit, or ill-temper, righteous indignation ; bring it to the light, come face to face with it, confess it and get it cleansed away.

" And they that are Christ's have crucified the flesh with the affections and lusts." When a man is saved his human nature is not altered ; human nature is marred by sin, but it is not bad. Deliverance from sin does not mean deliverance from human nature. By regeneration a man is perfectly adjusted to God, now he is required to do a man's bit, viz.: to take his human nature and make it serve the new disposition. The honour of Jesus Christ is at stake in my bodily life, and if I walk in the Spirit I will be ruthless to the things that won't submit to Him. To " crucify the flesh with the affections and lusts " is not God's business, it is man's.

" And afterward that which is spiritual." We are made partakers of the Divine nature through the promises (see 2 Peter i, 4), the inherent tendency of the Divine nature is implanted in us through regeneration and we become children of God; we become, that is, not only what we are by nature, creations of God, but sons and daughters of God, with a strong family likeness to Jesus. The true conception of Man is our Lord. Man got out of God's order, and we are brought back not merely into the original order, but into a much better position through our Lord, viz.: we are to be " conformed to the image of His Son." We look at the things that are expressed externally; God looks at the tendency born in us. He knows, apart from all our pious phrases and pretences, whether we have been regenerated, He sees what the life will become. Browning puts it as no other writer outside the Bible:

> *All I could never be,*
> *All, men ignored in me.*
> *—This, I was worth to God,*

DISCOVERING GOD

1. *Evangelical v. Eclectic Expression.*

The effort is on an individual and philanthropic scale, not on a world scale, an evangelical scale—it is unequal to the world crisis. . . . It is the climax of a generation of genial and gentle religion, with the nerve of the Cross cut, which

*therefore breaks in our hands at a great historic crisis for lack
of the moral note—tonic, radical, and redemptive.*

FORSYTH.

Evangelical—the belief that God was " manifested in the
flesh " in the Person of His Son in order that through
His death on the Cross men might be redeemed. The
Apostle Paul sums up evangelical belief when he says—
" For He hath made Him to be sin for us, who knew no
sin ; that we might be made the righteousness of God in
Him " : that is, Jesus Christ takes my heredity of sin,
and gives me His own heredity of holiness, and I show the
alteration through my skin. The emphasis is apt to be put
on one phase only, viz.: justification by faith ; the real
centre of the action of the Redemption has to do with a
man's ruling disposition. If a man takes the rational common-
sense line he despises the evangelical view, but when he
gets down to things as they are he finds that the rational
view is on the fifteenth storey and the evangelical view is
at the basis. The rational view misses out the fact that there
is an hiatus between God and man ; things are wild, there
is a tragedy, something irrational not rational, at the heart
of life and the way out is not by reason, but only through
the Cross of Christ. These things are fundamental, they
come straight home to the problems of a man's own heart
and life. The point for me is, Do I agree with God in what
He condemns in the Cross ? That is where most of our
Christianity is proved to be humbug. We believe in what
we call the plan of salvation, but we don't do much else.
We ought to be busy *thinking* as Christians. Up to the
time of the war religious people were taken up, not so much
with the fundamental revelation of the Redemption as with
expounding a certain type of saintliness, a particular pre
sentation of the Gospel, consequently when the war struck

they were not able to grasp the providential order of God at all, they were found enervated, " unequal to the world crisis."

2. *Temperamental v. True Portrayal.*

God so loved, so unsparingly, as to do His Son's body and soul the injury of the Cross. That is the principle on which God's love dealt with the vast evil of the world. He reserved for Himself what He forbade Abraham to do.   FORSYTH.

Temperamental—the way a man looks at life. My temperament is an inner disposition which influences my thoughts and actions to a certain extent, i.e., I am either pessimistic or optimistic according to the way my blood circulates. It is an insult to take the temperamental line in dealing with a human being—" Cheer up, look on the bright side " ; there are some types of suffering before which the only thing you can do is to keep your mouth shut. There are times when a man needs to be handled by God, not by his fellow men, and part of the gift of man's wisdom is to know how to be reverent with what he does not understand.

To take the temperamental view of Jesus Christ will mean that I do not make the revelation of the Bible my guide, I portray Him as one who lived beyond His age and suffered in consequence ; all He did was to leave us a good example which we must try to follow, so that when a man makes the supreme sacrifice and lays down his life, he thereby redeems his own soul. A more hopeless misunderstanding of the Redemption could not be. When a man lays down his life, it takes God to expound what he has done. " Greater love hath no man than this, that a man lay down his life for his friends." The love of God is seen in that He laid

down His life for His enemies. The Redemption is God's
" bit." " None of them can by any means redeem his brother,
nor give to God a ransom for him : (for the redemption
of their soul is costly, and must be left alone for ever)"
(Psalm xlix, 7, 8).

What Forsyth is pointing out is that the temperamental
view ignores the fact that God deliberately paid the price
of dealing with sin. It is easy if I reason from the logical
common-sense point of view, to say that God created the
man who became a sinner, and then condemns him to hell
because he sinned. The Bible says nothing of the sort.
The Bible says that God Himself accepted the responsibility for sin ; the Cross is the proof that He did. It cost
Jesus Christ to the last drop of blood to deal with " the
vast evil of the world." The true portrayal is that the Cross
is not the cross of a man, but the Cross of God. The tragedy
of the Cross is the hurt to God. In the Cross God and sinful
man merge ; consequently the Cross is of more importance
than all the world's civilisations.

" He that spared not His own Son, but delivered Him up
for us all, how shall He not with Him also freely give us
all things ? " What does that mean ? It means that I can
receive a new disposition the second I see my need—
" If ye then, being evil, know how to give good gifts unto
your children, how much more shall your heavenly Father
give the Holy Spirit to them that ask Him ? " It is so
simple that the majority of us blunder over it, we won't
come the bairn way ; but when a man is up against things
the words of Jesus become the deepest philosophy in life—
" Come unto Me " ; " Believe also in Me." My relation
to things proves whether or not I do believe in Jesus. The
life of a child of God is always the life of a child, simple
and open-hearted, no ulterior motive. The Bible makes
more of the death of Jesus than of His life and His teaching,

because the teaching of Jesus does not apply to you and me unless we have received His Spirit. What is the good of telling me to love my enemies ? I hate them ! to be fathomlessly pure in heart ? to have no unworthy motive ? The teaching of Jesus is for the life He puts in, and I receive that life by means of the Cross.

3. *Dogmatic Creed v. Deity of Christ.*

No man begins his Christian life by believing a creed. The man with a dogmatic creed says, " You must believe this and that." Jesus says, " Do the will," i.e., " commit yourself to Me." Truth is not in a particular statement ; Truth is a Person, " I am the Truth." It is a mistake to attempt to define what a man must believe before he can be a Christian ; his beliefs are the effect of his being a Christian, not the cause of it. Immediately you lose sight of the central, majestic Figure of Jesus Christ you are swept off your feet by all kinds of doctrine, and when big things hit you find your religion does not stand you in good stead because your creed does not agree with the Truth.

The revelation of the Deity of Christ does not come first to a man's intellect, but to his heart and life, and he says with amazement, " Thou art the Christ, the Son of the living God." The great point of the Bible revelation of God is not only that God was *in* Christ, but that Jesus Christ *is* God. If Jesus Christ is not God, then the only God we have is an abstraction of our own minds. I know no other God in Time or Eternity than Jesus Christ ; I have accepted all I know of God on the authority of the revelation He gave of Him. " He that hath seen Me hath seen the Father."

We never discover God until we come to a personal need for Him, and that drives us to Jesus. The whole meaning of life is that a man discovers God for himself. It is not sin that keeps us away from Jesus, but our own goodness.

" I am not come to call the righteous," Jesus said, " but sinners to repentance." We don't seem to need God until we come up against things. The basis for thinking with most of us is our ordinary logical common-sense, but when a man comes up against things he has to go deeper down than his common-sense, to fall back on something else, either fatalism or God. The Christian thought is not fatalistic, it is based on the revelation of God given by Jesus Christ.

COMMON CHRISTIAN THINKING

1. *The Divine Unction of Christian Teaching.*

But ye have an unction from the Holy One, and ye know all things. I JOHN ii, 20.

The Apostle John in these verses does away with the idea that there are specialists in Christian thinking as there are specialists in other domains ; he says, No, the Holy Spirit is the one Teacher, and the teaching He imparts is common to us all, consequently there is no excuse for any of us, no room for saying, " I haven't had a good education " ; " I haven't had time to study." The majority of us recognise the necessity of receiving the Holy Spirit for living, but we do not sufficiently recognise the need for drawing on the resources of the Holy Spirit for thinking. Many of us don't realise that we *can* think, we lie all abroad in our minds, wool-gathering. When we receive the Holy Spirit He imparts the ability to see things by intuition. Spiritual intuition lives in the same sphere as natural intuition *plus* the Holy Spirit.

> *I do not like thee, Dr. Fell,*
> *The reason why I cannot tell ;*
> *But this I know, and know full well—*
> *I do not like thee, Dr. Fell.*

That is natural intuition, i.e., instant perception of the truth of things without reasoning or analysis. Instruction in spiritual intuition is what we need. The Holy Spirit will curb and check natural intuition until He brings it into accord with what Jesus meant when He said, " My sheep hear My voice." When you listen to a preacher, how are you going to know whether he is teaching the truth of God ? Only by spiritual intuition. You may know that God has wonderfully used a man in the past, but never make that your ground for heeding what he says now, for at any minute a man may be out of touch with God. (cf. 1 Corinthians ix, 27.) Never pin your faith to a man's reputation as a servant of God, always watch for the Holy Spirit. If a man is talking the truth of God those who listen will meet it again whether they like it or not ; if he is not talking God's truth they won't come across it any more. Whenever the grand simple sanity of the Holy Spirit's interpretation is wanting, hold the matter in abeyance. The one stamp of the right interpretation is its " warm " natural sanity, it is not fantastic or peculiar, it doesn't twist your brain, it makes you feel, How marvellously simple and beautiful that is !

The Holy Spirit's anointing abides " in you," says John. At the beginning of your spiritual life you wanted to run off to this man and that, to this book and that, until you learn that " the anointing abideth in you." John and Paul and Peter all insist on the superb right of the humblest believer to test the teacher by the anointing which is in him. If we put teachers over against the Holy Ghost, when God removes them we go down, we mourn and say, " What shall we do now ? " Watch how Paul deals with the people who say, " I am of Paul ; and I of Apollos ; and I of Cephas " ; he says in effect, " All teachers are yours." A teacher is simply meant to rouse us up to face the truths revealed in the Bible and witnessed to by the Holy Ghost. Watch the tendency which is in us all to try and safeguard God's truth. The remarkable thing is that God never safeguards His own truth ; He leaves statements in this Book we can easily misrepresent, the only test is the Holy Spirit who leads us into all truth.

" And ye need not that any man teach you." It is here that Satan comes in as an angel of light and says, If you are anointed by the Spirit, everything you think is right. Not at all. Only as we obey the Spirit and keep in the light does the anointing abide. Our thinking and common-sense reasoning must be rigorously subordinated to the Spirit, and if we abide true to Him He repairs the damage sin has done to conscience and mind and keeps our thinking vital and true. Notice in your own life how He works. He begins with the big general principles and then slowly educates you down to the scruple.

2. *The Divine Union of Christian Thinking.*

But as the same anointing teacheth you of all things. I JOHN ii, 27.

We have perenially to rely on the one great Source of all teaching, viz. : the Holy Spirit ; He puts us in an independent position towards all other teachers, and makes our dependence on Himself as the one Teacher the only basis of union there is, " the unity of the Spirit." " There is one body, one Spirit . . . one Lord, one faith, one baptism." *Be filled with the Spirit*, says Paul. We have all seen the seashore when the tide is out, with all its separate pools, how are those pools to be made one ? By digging channels between them ? No, wait till the tide comes in, and where are the pools ? Absolutely lost, merged in one tremendous floodtide. That is exactly what happens when Christians

D

are indwelt by the Holy Spirit. Once let people be filled with the Holy Spirit and you have the ideal of what the New Testament means by the Church. The Church is a separated band of people who are united to God by the regenerating power of the Spirit, and the bedrock of membership in the Church is that we know who Jesus is by a personal revelation of Him. The indwelling Spirit is the supreme Guide, and He keeps us absorbed with our Lord. The emphasis to-day is placed on the furtherance of an organisation; the note is, "We must keep this thing going." If we are in God's order the thing will go; if we are not in His order, it won't. Think of the works that are kept on after God wanted to rule them out of the way because they have a source of inspiration apart from Himself.

"Ye shall abide in Him." The test that we are being taught by the Holy Spirit is that our lives are proving identical with the life of the Son of God. You cannot have identity without individuality. False teaching says we lose our personality; we never do. Jesus Christ emancipates personality, and He makes individuality pronounced; but it is personality absolutely free from my right to myself, free from identity with any other personality, manifesting a strong family likeness to Jesus, and the transfiguring element is love to Himself.

The Psychology of Faith

I

I. *THE CONSTITUTION OF FAITH*

And without faith it is impossible to be well-pleasing unto Him. HEBREWS xi, 6, R.V.

There is not possible a normal healthy human being apart from religious faith. Faith claims the whole man and all God's grace can make him. FORSYTH.

THE conception of faith given in the New Testament is that it must embrace the whole man. Faith is not a faculty, faith is the whole man rightly related to God by the power of the Spirit of Jesus. We are apt to apply faith to certain domains of our lives only—we have faith in God when we ask Him to save us, or ask Him for the Holy Spirit, but we trust something other than God in the actual details of our lives. " Faith claims the whole man and all that God's grace can make him," just as it claimed the whole of our Lord's life. Our Lord represents the normal man, not the average man, but the man according to God's norm. His life was not cut up into compartments, one part sacred and another secular, it was not in any way a mutilated life. Jesus Christ was concentrated on one line, viz., the will of His Father, in every detail of His life. That is the normal standard for each of us, and the miracle of the Gospel is that He can put us into the condition where we can grow into the same image. Our Lord lived His

life not in order to show how good He was, but to give us
the normal standard for our lives. The life He lived is made
ours by means of His death; by the gift of the Holy Spirit
and obedience to Him, we are put into the relationship to
God that Jesus had—" that they may be one, even as We
are one."

Faith is a tremendously active principle of trust in Jesus
which is ready to venture on every word He speaks : " Lord,
Thou hast said " (e.g., Matthew vi, 33, " But seek ye first
the Kingdom of God and His righteousness ; and all these
things shall be added unto you "), " it looks mad, but I
am going to venture on it ; I will sink or swim on Thy
word." We cannot have faith in every word of Jesus whenever we think we will. The Holy Spirit brings a word of
Jesus to our remembrance and applies it to the circumstances
we are in, and the point is, will we obey that particular
word ? We may have seen Jesus and known His power
and yet never have ventured out in faith on Him. Faith
must be tested because only through conflict can head-
faith be turned into a personal possession. Faith according
to Jesus must have its object real, no one can worship an
ideal. We cannot have faith in God unless we know Him
in Jesus Christ. God is a mere abstraction to our outlook
until we see Him in Jesus and hear Him say, " He that
hath seen Me hath seen the Father," then we have something to build upon and faith becomes boundless.

2. FAITH AND CONFUSING ISSUES

Even so faith, if it hath not works, is dead, being alone.
JAMES ii, 17–20.

An inadequate theory of faith distorts practice. FORSYTH.

The Apostle James continually says, " If you have faith,
prove it by your life." Experience is never the ground of

my faith; experience is the evidence of my faith. Many
of us have had a marvellous experience of deliverance
from sin and of the baptism of the Holy Ghost, not a
fictional experience, but a real experience whereby we
prove to our amazement every day that God has delivered
us, then comes the danger that we pin our faith to our
experience instead of to Jesus Christ, and if we do, faith
becomes distorted. When the baptism of the Holy Ghost
came upon the early disciples it made them the written
epistles of what they taught, and it is to be the same with
us. Our experience is the proof that our faith is right.
Jesus Christ is always infinitely mightier than our faith,
mightier than our experience, but our experience will be
along the line of the faith we have in Him. Have we faith
to bear this testimony to those who know us—that we are
what we are because of our faith in Jesus? We have faith
in Jesus to save us, but do we prove that He has saved us by
living a new life? I say I believe that Jesus can do this and
that; well, has He done it? "But by the grace of God
I am what I am." Are we monuments of the grace of God,
or do we only experience God's supernatural power in our
work for Him? Extraordinary spiritual experiences spring
from something wrong in the life, you never get the ex-
quisite simple faith in God along any special line of experience, but only along the common line of regeneration
through faith in Jesus. Be sceptical of any revelation that
has not got as its source the simplicity by means of which
a " babe " can enter in, and which a " fool " can express.

3. FAITH AND CONSECRATED ISSUES

. . . *work out your own salvation.* PHILIPPIANS ii, 12–13.

*The normal course of all religious experience is expansion
followed by concentration.*   FORSYTH.

When God gives a vision of what sanctification means, or what the life of faith means, we have instantly to pay for the vision, and we pay for it by the inevitable law that " expansion must be followed by concentration." That means we must concentrate on the vision until it becomes real. Over and over again the vision is mistaken for the reality. God's great Divine anticipation can only be made manifest by our human participation, these two must not be put asunder. Every expansion of brain and heart that God gives in meetings or in private reading of the Bible must be paid for inevitably and inexorably by concentration on our part, not by consecration. God will continually bring us into circumstances to make us prove whether we will work out with determined concentration what He has worked in. If you have had a vivid religious experience of the baptism of the Holy Ghost, what are you going to do with it ? We are sanctified by God's grace and made one with Jesus in order that we might sanctify our holiness to God as Jesus did. " And for their sakes I sanctify Myself," (John xvii, 19). There is no difficulty in getting sanctified if my will and affections have at their heart the earnest desire for God's glory. If I am willing for God to strangle in me the thing that makes me everlastingly hanker after my own point of view, my own interests, my own whiteness —if I am willing for all that to be put to death, then " the God of peace will sanctify me wholly." Sanctification means a radical and absolute identification with Jesus until the springs of His life are the springs of my life. " Faithful is He that calleth you, who also will do it."

The great need to-day is for Christians to toe the line : " And the heathen shall know that I am the Lord, saith the Lord God, *when I shall be sanctified in you before their eyes* (Ezekiel xxxvi, 23). Unless Christians are facing up to God's commands there is no use pushing forward to meet the life of our time. Jesus wants us to face the life of our time in the power of the Holy Ghost. Do we proclaim by our lives, by our thinking, by our faith in God, that Jesus Christ is sufficient for every problem life can present? that there is no force too great for Him to cope with and overcome? If our faith is not living and active it is because we need reviving; we have a faith that is limited by certain doctrines instead of being " the faith of God."

The Apostle Paul is always tremendously practical, he comes right down to where we live, he says we must *work out* the salvation God has *worked in*. " All power is given unto Me," said Jesus, and by the Holy Spirit's presence we can do those things which please God—are we doing them? By the power of the indwelling Holy Spirit we can bring every thought and imagination into captivity to the obedience of Christ, and can keep this body the chaste temple of the Holy Ghost—are we doing it? By the power of the Holy Spirit we can keep our communications with other people the exact expression of what God is working in us—are we doing it? The proof that we have a healthy vigorous faith is that we are expressing it in our lives, and bearing testimony with our lips as to how it came about.

There is no end to the life of faith; sanctification itself is only the ABC of the Christian life. The life of Jesus from Bethlehem onwards is a picture of the sanctified life, and anything that would make our souls stagnate produces a distortion. It is a continual learning, but not of the same lesson, if we have to be taught the same lesson it is because we have been very stupid. God will bring us into circumstances and make us learn the particular lessons He wants us to learn, and slowly and surely we will work out all that He works in. There is no patience equal to the patience of God.

The Psychology of Faith

1. *FAITH AND THE SON OF GOD*

. . . looking unto Jesus the author and perfecter of our faith. HEBREWS xii, 2, R.V.

He fought the battle, He proved the possibility of victory, He shewed us the place and revealed to us the secret of the power. FORSYTH.

Jesus Christ is the Captain of our faith ; He has gained the victory, consequently for us Satan is a conquered foe. When we are sanctified and have become " His brethren " we are put, not in the place of the first Adam, but in the place of the last Adam, where we live by the power and might of the faith of the Son of God. We have to get rid of the idea that because Jesus was God He could not be tempted. Almighty God cannot be tempted, but in Jesus Christ we deal with God as man, a unique Being—God-Man. It was as Son of Man that " He fought the battle, and proved the possibility of victory." After His Baptism, Satan, by the direct permission of the Holy Ghost, tested the faith of Jesus. (" And straightway the Spirit driveth Him forth into the wilderness." Mark i, 12.) Satan broke what Adam held straight off, but he could not break what Jesus held in His Person though he tested Him in every conceivable way ; therefore having Himself suffered being tempted, " He is able to succour them that are tempted."

When we are born again we get our first introduction into what God calls temptation. When we are sanctified we are not delivered from temptation, we are loosened into it ; we are not free enough before either morally or spiritually to be tempted. Immediately we become His " brethren " we are free, and all these subleties are at work. God does not shield any man or woman from any requirements of a full-grown man or woman. Luke xxii, 28 (" But ye are they which have continued with Me in My temptations ") presents Our Lord's view of His life as Man, viz., as one of temptations, not triumphs. When we are born again the Son of God is submitted to temptations in our individual lives, are we remaining loyal to Him in His temptations in us ? When temptation comes, stand absolutely true to God no matter what it costs you, and you will find the onslaught leaves you with affinities higher and purer than ever before. Temptation overcome is the transfiguration of the natural into the spiritual and the establishment of conscious affinity with the purest and best.

2. FAITH AND THE SONS OF GOD

Beloved, now are we the sons of God. 1 JOHN iii, 2.

Having been made sons of God does not absolve us from the lifelong task of actually making ourselves sons of God.

FORSYTH.

We have to take pains to make ourselves what God has taken pains to make us. You can take a horse to the trough, but you can't make him drink ; you can send your child to school, but you can't make him study ; and God can put a saint into a right relationship with Himself, but He cannot make him work out that relationship, the saint must do that himself. We must take the pains to make ourselves visibly all that God has made us invisibly. God alters our disposition, but He does not make our character. When God alters my disposition the first thing the new disposition will do is to stir up my brain to think along God's line. As I begin to think, begin to work out what God has worked in, it will become character. Character is consolidated thought. God makes me pure in heart; I must make myself pure in conduct. This point of working things out in actuality is apt to be lost sight of.

The business of faith is to convert Truth into reality. What do you really believe? take time and catalogue it up; are you converting your belief into reality? You say, " I believe God has sanctified me "—does your actual life prove He has? " I believe God has baptized me with the Holy Ghost "—why? Because you had cold shivers and visions and marvellous times of prayer? The proof that we are baptized with the Holy Ghost is that we bear a strong family likeness to Jesus, and men take knowledge of us, as they did of the disciples after Pentecost, that we have been with Jesus, they recognize the family likeness at once. True justification can only result in sanctification. By justification God anticipates that we are holy in His sight, and if we will obey the Holy Spirit we will prove in our actual life that God is justified in justifying us. Ask yourself—Is God justified in my justification? do I prove by the way I live and talk and do my work that God has made me holy? Am I converting God's purpose in justifying me into actual experience, or only delighting in God's anticipation? There is a great snare especially in evangelical circles of knowing the will of God as expressed in the Bible without the slightest practical working of it out in the life. The Christian religion is the most practical thing on earth. If the Holy Spirit has given you a vision in your private Bible study or during a meeting which made your heart glow, and your mind expand, and your will stir itself to grasp, you will have to pay to the last farthing in concentration along that line until all you saw in vision is made actual. During these past years there has been a terrific expansion in lives through bereavement and sorrow, everything in individual life has been altered, but there is the price to pay. The price is the same in national as in individual life.

The peculiar aspect of religious faith is that it is faith in a Person who relates us to Himself and commits us to His point of view, not faith in a point of view divorced from relationship to a Person. "If you would know My doctrine," said Jesus, "do My will." Our Lord never teaches first by principles, but by personal relationship to Himself. When through His Redemption we become rightly related to Him personally, our hearts are unshakeably confident in Him. That is the Divine anticipation being participated in, the tremendous work of God's supernatural grace being manifested in our mortal flesh.

The Psychology of Faith

III

1. *MENTAL BELIEF*

But as many as received Him, to them gave He power to become the sons of God, even to them that believe on His name. JOHN i, 12, 13.

John i, 12, 13 is a grand, mighty, all-embracing word— " to as many as *received* Him . . . " The way mental belief works is that it leads us to understand who Jesus Christ is and what He can do for us and in us. Jesus Christ is the normal Man, the Man according to God's standard, and God demands of us the very holiness He exhibited.

A spiritually minded Christian has to go through the throes of a total mental readjustment ; it is a God-glorifying process, if a humbling one. People continually say, " How can I have more faith ? " You may ask for faith to further orders, but you will never have faith apart from Jesus Christ. You can't pump up faith out of your own heart. Whenever faith is starved in your soul it is because you are not in contact with Jesus ; get in contact with Him and lack of faith will go in two seconds. Whenever Jesus Christ came across people who were free from the ban of finality which comes from religious beliefs, He awakened faith in them at once. The only ones who were without faith in Him were those who were bound up by religious certitude. Faith means that I commit myself to Jesus, project myself

absolutely on to Him, sink or swim—and you do both,
you sink out of yourself and swim into Him. Faith is
implicit confidence in Jesus and in His faith. It is one thing
to have faith in Jesus and another thing to have faith about
everything for which He has faith. Galatians ii, 20 does
not refer to the Apostle Paul's elementary faith in Jesus
as his Saviour, but to the faith of Jesus. He says that the
identical faith that was in Jesus Christ, the faith that
governed His life, the faith which Satan could not break,
is now in him through identification with the death of Jesus ;
the faith that characterized Him now characterizes Paul.

2. *MORAL BELIEF*

*Knowing this, that our old man is crucified with Him, that
the body of sin might be destroyed, that henceforth we should
not serve sin.* ROMANS vi, 6.

If we are honest and obedient, moral belief will follow
mental belief very quickly. Am I poor enough, humble
enough, and simple enough to believe in Jesus ? Do I
believe Him when He says that God will give me the Holy
Spirit if I ask Him ? If I do believe in Jesus and receive the
Holy Spirit on the authority of His word, then I will have
to make a moral decision about all that the Holy Spirit
reveals. He will reveal to me what sin is, and He will
reveal that Jesus Christ can deliver me from sin if I will
agree with God's verdict on it in the Cross. Many of us
do believe in Jesus, we have received the Holy Spirit and
know we are children of God, and yet we won't make the
moral decision about sin, viz., that it must be killed right
out in us. It is the great moment of our lives when we decide
that sin must die right out, not be curbed or suppressed
or counteracted, but crucified. It is not done easily ; it
is only done by a moral wrench. We never understand

the relation between a human life and the Cross of Christ until we perform a moral act and have the light of God thrown upon realities.

The transactions which tell in my life for God are moral decisions, not mental ones. I may think through everything there is in Christian doctrine and yet remain exactly the same; but I never make a moral decision and remain the same, and it is the moral decisions to which the Holy Spirit is always leading us on the basis of the Redemption. A moral decision is not a decision that takes time, one second is sufficient; what takes time is my stubborn refusal to come to the point of morally deciding. Here, where we sit, we can decide whether or not the Redemption shall take its full course in us. Once I decide that it shall, the great inrush of the Redemption takes efficacious effect immediately. There are times when the Holy Spirit does touch us, times when there are " flashes struck from midnight " and we see everything clearly, and that is where the danger comes in, because we are apt to let those touches pass off in senti-mental ardour instead of making a moral decision. It is a sensible delight to feel God so near, but unless a moral decision is made you will find it much harder next time to pay attention to the touch when it comes. It is better to decide without the accompaniment of the glow and the thrill—better to decide in cold blood, when your own will is in the ascendant, deliberately swayed by the rulership of Christ.

3. *MYSTIC BELIEF*

For ye are dead, and your life is hid with Christ in God. COLOSSIANS iii, 3.

Paul is not talking to disembodied spirits, he is talking to men and women who have been through identification with the death of Jesus and know that their " old man "

is crucified with Him. If we are born again of the Holy
Ghost, and have made the moral decision to obey what He
reveals about sin, then we must go on to believe that God
can enable us to live for His glory in any circumstances He
places us in. You can always detect the right kind of belief
in Jesus by a flesh-and-blood testimony. "Wherefore ye
shall know them by their fruits." Other people are not
likely to confuse grapes with thorns, or figs with thistles.
Mystic belief means that we enter into a conscious inheritance
of what the Redemption has wrought for us, and daily, hourly,
manifest the marvel of the grace of God in our actual lives.
The majority of us "hang on" to Jesus Christ, we are
thankful for the massive gift of salvation, but we don't do
anything towards working it out. That is the difficult bit,
and the bit the majority of us fail in, because we have not
been taught that that is what we have to do, consequently
there is a gap between our religious profession and our
actual practical living. To put it down to human frailty is
a wiggle, there is only one word for it, and that is "humbug."
In my actual life I live below the belief which I profess.
We can do nothing towards our salvation, but we can work
out what God works in and the emphasis all through the
New Testament is that God gives us sufficient energy to
do it if we will. The great factor in Christian experience is
the one our Lord continually brought out, viz., the reception
of the Holy Spirit who does *in* us what He did *for* us, and
slowly and surely our natural life is transformed into a
spiritual life through obedience.

Notes on Lamentations

THE Lamentations are not the expression of the grief of a disappointed man, the peculiar element in Jeremiah's sorrow is that he is identifying himself with an unrepentant people. (Cf. Daniel ix, 4–20.) We suffer on account of our own wrong or the wrong of others, but that is not vicarious suffering. Jeremiah's grief personifies vicariously the grief of the whole nation. Am I prepared to be a scapegoat for the sins of others for which they are still unrepentant ?

CHAPTER I—Elegy in Degradation.

How doth the city sit solitary, that was full of people ! . . . she weepeth sore in the night, and her tears are on her cheeks. vv. 1–2.

The city herself is introduced weeping, and giving expression to her sorrow over the evil determined against her on account of her sins.

"How doth the city sit solitary." Being alone is not solitariness ; solitariness is loneliness that has in it an element of moral dis-esteem : "Jerusalem hath grievously sinned ; therefore she is become as an unclean thing : all that honoured her despise her." (v. 8). Cain's solitariness is typical of this loneliness ; so is the loneliness of the prodigal son in the far country who starved on what the pigs throve on. Man was not created to be alone. Jesus Christ was rarely alone ; the times when He was alone are distinctly stated. Solitariness to be beneficial must never be sought and must never be on account of sin. If I choose solitariness, I go back into active life with annoyance and a contempt for other people, proving that my seeking solitariness was selfish.

" He hath spread a net for my feet . . . " (v. 13). There is no choice after the choice is made, we are at the mercy of God's inexorable justice once the choice is made which leads " into the net." Our destiny is not determined for us, but it is determined by us. Man's free will is part of God's sovereign will. We have freedom to take which course we choose, but not freedom to determine the end of that choice. God makes clear what He desires, we must choose, and the result of the choice is not the inevitableness of law, but the inevitableness of God. Verse 18 gives the reason for all that is happening—" The Lord is righteous ; for I have rebelled against His commandment." God will never change His character to please anyone's pleading or petulance if they have deliberately spurned His counsel.

There are irreparable losses in human life, and no amount of whining will alter it. The Garden of Eden was closed, not to naughty children, but to sinners, and is never again opened to sinners. " The way of the tree of life " is guarded, preventing man getting back as a sinner ; he only gets back, and thank God he does get back, in and through the Redemption. What is prophesied with regard to Jerusalem is the attitude of the Spirit of God to the human race. The attitude of those not indwelt by the Spirit of God is that man's capabilities are a promise of what he is going to be : the Holy Ghost sees man as a ruin of what he once was. He does not delight in his natural virtues. We are being told what a splendid race of human beings we are !—we are a race of rebels, and the rebellion has got to be destroyed. When the Holy Ghost is having His way with a man the

E

first thing He does is to corrupt confidence in virtues which belong to a ruin. Nothing is more highly esteemed among men than pride in my virtues, i.e., self-realization, but Jesus Christ said that " that which is highly esteemed among men is an abomination in the sight of God." If this was realized we would understand the extravagant language of Scripture about sin.

CHAPTER II—Elegy in Destruction.

How hath the Lord covered the daughter of Zion with a cloud in His anger! He hath cast down from heaven unto the earth the beauty of Israel . . . vv. 1–2.

The prophets of God have always one burden when they deal with the judgments of God, and that is that they come not from the east, nor from the west, but are directly stamped as " from the Lord." The tendency to-day is to put the consequences of sin as natural consequences : the consequences of sin have a righteous God behind them. We have taken the Bible idea out of punishment and say, " Oh well, it is the inevitable result " ; the Bible says the inevitable result is brought about by a personal God.

" The Lord is become as an enemy . . . " (v. 5). Deliverance comes through destruction, and for a while the soul does not know whether God is a friend or an enemy. God has one purpose in destruction, and that is the deliverance of His own. God's own is not *you*, but His own *in you*. All that is saved is the work of God in a man, nothing else. Destruction means the obliteration of every characteristic of the life that is not rooted in godliness, it never means the annihilation of the life. The judgments of God are a consuming fire whereby He destroys in order to deliver ; the time to be alarmed in life is when all things are undisturbed. The knowledge that God is a consuming fire is the greatest comfort to the saint, it is His love at work on those characteristics that are not true to godliness. The saint who is near to God knows no burning, but the farther away from God the sinner gets, the more the fire of God burns him.

In vv. 1-9 the wrath of God is emphasized. God's love is wrath towards wrong; He is never tender to that which hates goodness. All through the Bible reveals that when once communion with God is severed the basis of life is chaos and wrath. The chaotic elements may not show themselves at once, but they will presently. All that this Book says about corruption in connection with the flesh is as certain as God is on His throne if the life is not rightly related to God. When we speak of the wrath of God we must not picture Him as an angry sultan on the throne of heaven, bringing a lash about people when they do what He does not want. There is no element of personal vindictiveness in God. It is rather that God's constitution of things is such that when a man becomes severed from God his life tumbles into turmoil and confusion, into agony and distress, it is hell at once, and he will never get out of it unless he turns to God; immediately he turns, chaos is turned into cosmos, wrath into love, distress into peace. "Knowing therefore the terror of the Lord" we persuade men to keep in touch with Him. The world pays no attention to those who tell them how God convicted of sin and how He delivered them; the warnings of God are of no use to sinners until they are convicted of sin and the warnings become applicable to them.

"The elders of the daughter of Zion sit upon the ground, they keep silence." (v. 10.) When God's destructions are abroad there is no power to move, only to sit; no power to speak, only to keep silence. It is not a time for social intercourse of any kind, but for the deepest dejection.

" Mine eyes do fail with tears . . . for the destruction of the daughter of my people." No prophet stands so close to Jesus Christ as Jeremiah, he is the one who realizes human conditions more keenly than any other and identifies himself with them. Verses 11–19 are his lamentation over the impotence of human consolation.

" The prophets . . . have not discovered thine iniquity." (v. 14.) The prophet with a message based on human morality excuses sin instead of detecting it—" God knows you can't help this sort of thing "—that is a lie. " Under the circumstances you will be excused." Jeremiah was indignant with those prophets who gave a wrong application to God's message : " Sin is sin ; but you don't need to imagine that that is the reason for what God is doing " ; Jeremiah held to it that it was the reason.

" . . . the day of the Lord's anger." (vv. 20–22.) When God's limit is reached, He destroys into salvation ; He destroys the unsaveable and liberates the saveable. Judgment days are an overflowing mercy because they separate between right and wrong. To be experimental in me the salvation of Jesus Christ is always a judgment, and it brings the understanding of God's justice even in His severest judgments. If we compare our attitude with the revelations made in God's Book we find how despicably shallow we are. Our attitude is not one of sympathy of God, not a sensitive understanding of His point of view, only an amazing sensitiveness over our own calamities and those of other people, consequently we act on the principle of giving " a pill to cure an earthquake." When God is squeezing the life of a man or of a nation in order to save the remnant, what is the use of my coming and kicking at the fingers of God and saying, " I shan't allow You to do this ? " If our human sympathy with the one who is suffering under the hand of God is justified, then God is cruel. Some of us

are so set on our own honour that we have no time for
God's honour.

" Is this the city that men called The perfection of beauty?
The joy of the whole earth ? " (v. 15.) Jeremiah is referring
to the desolation which, by God's own decree, has fallen
on everything God made to be holy ; he sees God's judgment on His own choicest things—Jerusalem ruined, the
Temple destroyed. " See, O Lord, and behold, to whom
Thou hast done thus ! " (v. 20.) And Jeremiah's whole
heart was in Jerusalem ! God did not spare His people.
His judgment on them was as unconquerably certain as it
was on Babylon, and as it is on us. No amount of pleading
will ever alter the judgments of God.

CHAPTER III—*Elegy in Desolation.*

*Surely against me he turneth his hand again and again all
the day. . . . vv. 1–21.*

Obedience to God will mean that some time or other
you enter into desolation ; if you don't obey, you won't—
for a time. Jeremiah is speaking in vicarious terms of the
sorrow and anguish of the people under God's chastisement ;
he is not cutting a cross-section through his own personal
grief, not writing his own spiritual autobiography. Jeremiah
is a vicarious sufferer, that is, he does not find his place
in other people, he lets other people find their place in him.
Our attitude too often is—" Oh, that has nothing to do
with me, I have enough to bear." We will be of no use in
God's service until that spirit is removed. God so loves the
world that He hates the wrong in it. Do I so love men and
women that I hate the wrong in them ? Most of us love
other people for what they are to us instead of for what God
wants them to be. The distress worked in a man's heart by
the Holy Ghost is never on his own account, but always on
God's account.

Desperate tides of the whole great world's anguish
Forced thro' the channels of a single heart.

Have I ever shared for a moment God's concern over people,
or am I putting myself in a bandage before God and saying,
" I can't stand any more " ?

" Wherefore doth a living man complain, a man for the
punishment of his sins ? " (v. 39.) The judgments of God
leave scars, and the scars remain until I humbly and joy-
fully recognize that the judgments are deserved and that
God is justified in them. The last delusion God delivers us
from is the idea that we don't deserve what we get. Once
we see ourselves under the canopy of God's overflowing
mercy we are dissolved in wonder, love and praise. That
is the meaning of repentance, which is the greatest gift
God ever gives a man. As long as my heart has never been
broken by conviction of sin, I don't understand the Psalmist
when he says, " The sacrifices of God are a broken spirit :
a broken and a contrite heart, O God, Thou wilt not despise."
(Psalm li, 17.) When you get there God is the only Reality ;
but you only get there through heartbreak and sorrow.
Holiness is based on repentance, and the holy man is the
most humble man you can meet. My realization of God
can be measured by my humility.

Jeremiah's reliance on the justice of God breaks into a
prayer in which is manifested his confidence that God will
send help—" I called upon Thy name, O Lord, out of the
lowest dungeon. Thou heardest my voice ; hide not Thine
ear at my breathing, at my cry." (vv. 55–56.)

CHAPTER IV—*Elegy in Dispersion.*

*When they fled away and wandered, men said among the
nations, They shall no more sojourn here.* v. 15.

" How is the gold become dim ! How is the most pure

gold changed ! " (v. 1.) It is the holiest things that are
desolated. God ordained the Temple, Jerusalem was His
holy city, and yet He allows them to be ruined. Flesh and
blood, man's body, is meant to be " the temple of the
Holy Ghost "—God's " gold," but sin renders it disrepu-
table. The depth of possible sin is measured by the height
of possible holiness. When men come under conviction
of sin by the Holy Spirit their " beauty is consumed away,
like as it were a moth fretting a garment." The misery
which conviction brings enables a man to realize what God
created him for, viz., to glorify God and enjoy Him for ever.

" For the iniquity of the daughter of my people is greater
than the sin of Sodom, that was overthrown as in a moment."
(v. 6.) The destruction of Sodom was a sudden calamity ;
the destruction of Jerusalem was a terribly long, heart-
rending depreciation of everything of value in God's sight.

" It is because of the sin of her prophets, and the iniquities
of her priests, that have shed the blood of the just in the
midst of her." (v. 13.) Beware of iniquity, which means
conjuring yourself out of the straight ; finding out reasons
why you did not do what you know you should have done.
The term " iniquity " is used only of the people of God.
To " shed just blood " refers to more than actual murder.
The Bible never deals with proportionate sin ; according
to the Bible an impure thought is as bad as adultery ; a
covetous thought is as bad as a theft. It takes a long education in the things of God before we believe that is true.
Never trust innocence when it is contradicted by the word
of God. The tiniest bit of sin is an indication of the vast
corruption that is in the human heart. (" For from within,
out of the heart of man, proceed . . . " Mark vii, 21-23.)
That is why we must keep in the light all the time. Never
allow horror at crime to blind you to the fact that it is human
nature like your own that committed it. A saint is never

horror-stricken because although he knows that what our
Lord says about the human heart is true, he knows also
of a Saviour who can save to the uttermost.

"Thine iniquity hath an end." (v. 22, R.V. marg.) My
guilt is ended when I repent, when I stop admitting and begin
confessing. Am I blaming any of my forebears for my
present condition ? Then my punishment will go on till I
blame them no more. Am I blaming the circumstances in
which I live ? Then my punishment will go on till I stop
blaming my circumstances. As long as I have any remnant
of an idea that I can be cleared in any other way than by
God through the Redemption, my punishment will go on.
The instant I stop blaming everything but myself, and
acquit God of injustice to me, my recognition of Him begins.

CHAPTER V—*Elegy in Devotion.*

*Remember, O Lord, what is come upon us : behold, and see
our reproach.* v. 1.

What had Jeremiah done to deserve in the tiniest degree
all that has come upon him ? Nothing but obey God in
every detail, and because of his obedience he was in the
midst of the distress. The one man who has kept un-
spottedly right with God is in all the desolation, realizing
it more keenly than any of those who deserved it. A snare
spiritually is to refuse to "bear about in the body the
dying of Jesus," and prefer the gay hilarity which is only
possible for long in the new heaven and new earth. We
are here for one purpose : "to fill up that which is lacking of
the afflictions of Christ"—spoilt for this age, alive to
nothing but Jesus Christ's point of view. In this order of
things it is a maimed life, and few of us will have it ; we
prefer a full-orbed life of infinite satisfaction which makes
us absolutely crass to what is happening in "Jerusalem."

We can never be marked by the angel as those who sigh and cry for the sorrows of Jerusalem.

"Our fathers have sinned, and are not; and we have borne their iniquities." (v. 7.) These words are not to be understood as intimating that the speakers conceived themselves innocent—"Woe unto us! *for we have sinned.*" (v. 16.) The sins of the fathers are not visited on innocent children, but on children who continue the sins of their fathers (see Exodus xx, 5). Distinction must be made between punishment and suffering, they are not synonymous terms. A bad man's relation to his children is in God's hand : the child's relation to the badness of his father is in his own hand. Because we see children suffering physically for the sins of their parents, we say they are being punished; they are not, there is no element of punishment in their suffering; there are Divine compensations we know nothing about. The whole subject of heredity and what is transmitted by heredity, if taken out of its Bible setting, can be made the greatest slander against God, as well as the greatest exoneration of the bitterness of a man's spirit.

"The crown is fallen from our head ... for this our heart is faint; for these things our eyes are dim". (vv. 16–17). These words convey the poignancy of penitence. Nothing will make a man's heart " cave in " and his eyes stop seeing, saving sin. Sorrow won't do it, misfortune won't do it, hardship won't do it ; on the contrary these things, if there is no sin, make a man's heart strong. The " fallen crown " is the figurative expression for the honourable position of the people of God which they have now lost. Sin may make a man more desirable in the eyes of the world—" the sin which is admired of many " (Hebrews xii, 1, R.V. marg.), but what makes a man ugly physically, morally and spiritually is the discovery of sin by his own heart, and all attempts to justify himself spring from the depth of conviction of private sin.

The gathering in of God's salvation around a man means that he is checked at first by the merest zephyr touch, there is nothing so gentle as the check of the Holy Spirit ; if he obeys, emancipation is at once, if he does not obey, the zephyr touch will turn into a destructive blow from which there is no escape. There is never any shattering blow of God on the life that pays attention to the checks of the Spirit, but every time there is a spurning of the still small voice, the hardening of the life away from God goes on until destruction comes and shatters it. When I realize that there is something between God and me, it is at the peril of my soul I don't stop everything and get it put right. Immediately a thing makes itself conscious to me, it has no business there.

To sum up the Lamentations would be to say that the words of this vicarious sufferer direct the grieving human heart, in its deep sorrow, to the only true Comfort.

Duty of the Heart

And one of the scribes asked Him, Which is the first commandment of all? Mark xii, 28–34.

IN answering the scribe's question Our Lord does not say anything original, He takes two commandments from their place in the Old Testament, where they are obscured (see Deuteronomy vi, 5, Leviticus xix, 18) and brings them out into a startling light. "Think not," He said, "that I am come to destroy the law, or the prophets : I am not come to destroy, but to fulfil."

1. *Duty of Love for God.*

And thou shalt love the Lord thy God with all thy heart, and with all thy soul, and with all thy mind, and with all thy strength : this is the first commandment.

Where do we find ourselves with regard to this first great duty—"Thou shalt love the Lord thy God with all thy heart "? What does that phrase mean to us? If Jesus had said, "Thou shalt love thy lover with all thy heart," we would have known what He meant. Well, He did mean that, but the Lover is to be God. The majority of us have an ethereal, unpractical, bloodless abstraction which we call "love for God "; to Jesus love for God meant the most passionate intense love of which a human being is capable. The writer to the Hebrews states that Jesus Christ was "perfected through sufferings," but there is any amount of suffering that " im-perfects " us because it springs from unregulated passions. This fact has made some ethical teachers say that the passions themselves are evil, something human nature suffers from. Our Lord teaches that the passions are to be regulated by this first duty of love for God. The way we are to overcome the world, the flesh and the devil is by the force of our love for God regulating all our passions until every force of body, soul and spirit is devoted to this first great duty. This is the one sign of sanctification in a life ; any experience of santification which is less than that has something diseased about it.

If my first duty is to love God, the practical, sensible question to ask is, What is God like ? Aristotle taught that love for God does not exist ; " it is absurd to talk of such a thing, for God is an unknown being." The Apostle Paul met with the result of his teaching in his day—" Ye men of Athens . . . as I passed by, and beheld your devotions (the gods ye worship, marg.) I found an altar with this inscription TO THE UNKNOWN GOD. Whom therefore ye ignorantly worship, Him declare I unto you." (Acts xvii, 23.) To-day the teaching in many of our own colleges and universities is being honeycombed with pagan philosophy, pagan ethics, consequently there is a state of mind produced that appreciates what Aristotle said, that we cannot know God. Then what a startling statement Jesus made when He said, " Thou shalt love the Lord thy God with all thy heart " !

" No man hath seen God at any time ; the only begotten Son, which is in the bosom of the Father, He hath declared Him. (John i, 18.) Jesus knew God, and He makes Him known : " He that hath seen Me hath seen the Father." Get into the habit of recalling to your mind what Jesus was like when He was here, picture what He did and what He said, recall His gentleness and tenderness as well as His strength and sternness, and then say, " That is what God is like." I do not think it would be difficult for us to love Jesus if He went in and out among us as in the days of His flesh, healing the sick and diseased, restoring the distracted, putting right those who were wrong, reclaiming back-sliders—I do not think it would be difficult for us to love Him. That is to love God. The great Lover of God is the Holy Spirit, and when we receive the Holy Spirit we find we have a God whom we can know and whom we can love with all our heart because we see " the light of the knowledge of the glory of God in the face of Jesus Christ."

2. Duty of Love to Man.

And the second is like, namely this, Thou shalt love thy neighbour as thyself.

Everything our Lord taught about the duty of man to man might be summed up in the one law of giving. It is as if He set Himself to contradict the natural counsel of the human heart, which is to acquire and keep. A child will say of a gift, " Is it my own ? " When a man is born again that instinct is replaced by another, the instinct of giving. The law of the life of a disciple is Give, Give, Give, (e.g., Luke vi, 38). As Christians our giving is to be proportionate to all we have received of the infinite giving of God. " Freely ye have received, freely give." Not how much we give, but what we do not give, is the test of our Christianity. When we speak of giving we nearly always think only of money. Money is the life-blood of most of us. We have a remarkable trick—when we give money we don't give sympathy; and when we give sympathy we don't give money. The only way to get insight into the meaning for ourselves of what Jesus taught is by being indwelt by the Holy Spirit, because He enables us first of all to understand our Lord's life ; unless we do that, we will exploit His teaching, take out of it only what we agree with. There is one aspect of giving we think little about, but which had a prominent place in our Lord's life, viz., that of social intercourse. He accepted hospitality on the right hand and on the left, from publicans and from the Pharisees, so much so that they said He was " a gluttonous man, and a wine bibber, a friend of publicans and sinners ! " He spent Himself with one lodestar all the time, to seek and to save that which was lost, and Paul says, " I am become all things to all men, that I might by all means save some." How few of us ever think of giving socially ! We are so parsimonious that we won't spend a thing in conversation unless it is on a line that helps us !

And who is my neighbour ? (Luke x, 29.) Jesus gives an amazing reply, viz., that the answer to the question, " Who is my neighbour ? " is not to be found in the claim of the person to be loved, but in the heart of the one who loves. If my heart is right with God, every human being is my neighbour. There is engrained in the depths of human nature a dislike of the general ruck of mankind, in spite of all our modern jargon about " loving Humanity." We have a disparaging way of talking about the common crowd : the common crowd is made up of innumerable editions of you and me. Ask the Holy Spirit to enable your mind to brood for one moment on the value of the " nobody" to Jesus. The people who make up the common crowd are nobodies to me, but it is astonishing to find that it is the nobodies that Jesus Christ came to save. The terms we use for men in the sense of their social position are nothing to Him. There is no room in Christianity as Jesus Christ taught it for philanthropic or social patronage. Jesus Christ never patronised anyone, He came right straight down to where men live in order that the supreme gift He came to give might be theirs—" The Spirit of the Lord is upon

Me, because He hath anointed Me to preach the gospel to the poor." It is only by getting our mind into the state of the Mind of Jesus that we can understand how it is possible to fulfil the royal law and love our neighbour as ourselves. We measure our generosity by the standards of men ; Jesus says, " Measure your love for men by God's love for them, and if you are My disciple, you will love your neighbour *as I have loved you.*"

Holiness

---

1. *IMITATED*

. . . leaving us an example, that ye should follow His steps. I PETER ii, 21.

FOR one child to imitate another child only results in a more or less clever affectation ; a child imitating his parents assists the expression of inherent tendencies, naturally and simply, because he is obeying a nascent instinct. It is to this form of imitation that Peter alludes. When a saint imitates Jesus, he does it easily because he has the Spirit of Jesus in him. Pharisaic holiness, both ancient and modern, is a matter of imitation, seeking by means of prayer and religious exercises to establish, seriously and arduously, but un-regeneratedly, a self-determined holiness. The only spiritually holy life is a God-determined life. " Be ye holy ; for I am holy." If our best obedience, our most spotless moral walking, our most earnest prayers, are offered to God in the very least measure as the ground of our acceptance by Him, it is a fatal denial of the Atonement.

2. *IMPUTED*

. . . unto whom God imputeth righteousness without works. ROMANS iv, 6.

To impute means " to attribute vicariously " ; it is a theological word. The revelation made by the Apostle

Paul, viz., that God imputes righteousness to us, is the great truth at the basis of all our Protestant theology ; we are apt to forget this to-day. Righteousness means living and acting in accordance with right and justice, that is, it must express itself in a man's bodily life. " Little children, let no man deceive you : he that *doeth* righteousness is righteous." (1 John iii, 7). Imputed righteousness must never be made to mean that God puts the robe of His righteousness over our moral wrong, like a snow-drift over a rubbish heap ; that He pretends we are all right when we are not. The revelation is that " Christ Jesus is made unto us, righteousness " ; it is the distinct impartation of the very life of Jesus on the ground of the Atonement, enabling me to walk in the light as God is in the light, and as long as I remain in the light God sees only the perfections of His Son. We are " accepted in the Beloved."

3. *IMPARTED*

. . . not having a righteousness of mine own, but that which is through faith in Christ. PHILIPPIANS iii, 9.

The only holiness there is is the holiness derived through faith, and faith is the instrument the Holy Spirit uses to organize us into Christ. But do not let us be vague here. Holiness, like sin, is a disposition, not a series of acts. A man can *act* holily, but he has not a holy *disposition*. A saint has had imparted to him the disposition of holiness, therefore holiness must be the characteristic of the life here and now. Entire sanctification is the end of the disposition of sin, but only the beginning of the life of a saint, then comes growth in holiness. The process of sanctification begins at the moment of birth from above and is consummated on the unconditional surrender of my right to myself to Jesus Christ. The time that elapses between new birth

F

and entire sanctification depends entirely on the individual. Many souls have had such a blessed vision of an entirely sanctified life during Conventions, or in times of rare communion with God, that they imagine they have the reality, and it is at this stage that that subtle heresy, " Deeper death to self " is apt to lead them astray. The vision is followed by a deep valley of humiliation, by a cross of death, before the unspeakable reality is realized. If we have reached the stage of entire sanctification and have presented our bodies to be " a living sacrifice, holy, acceptable to God," what are we doing with our holy selves ? Jesus Christ gives us the key to the life of the saint—" And for their sakes I sanctify Myself." (John xvii, 19.) We are sanctified for one purpose only, that we might " sanctify our sanctification," i.e., deliberately give it to God.

4. *HABITUAL*

Be ye transformed by the renewing of your mind. ROMANS xii, 2.

Practical holiness is the only holiness of any value in this world, and the only kind the Spirit of God will endorse. If we consider what Professor James says in his scientific exposition of habit, it will be a great rebuke to our lazy neglect in finding out what we have to do to work out in actual life the holy disposition given us through the Atonement :

(a) *In the acquisition of a new habit, or the leaving off an old one, we must launch ourselves with as strong and decided initiative as possible.*

(b) *Never suffer an exception to occur till the new habit is securely rooted in your life.*

(c) *Seize the very first possible opportunity to act on every resolution you make, and on every emotional prompting you may experience in the direction of the habits you aspire to gain.*

Romans xii, 2 is the apostle Paul's passionate entreaty that we should rouse ourselves out of that stagnation which must end in degeneration, in which we are ensnared by thinking because it is " all of grace " there is no need for " gumption." Grace, Grit, Glory is the graduation course. Professor James says " we must launch ourselves with as strong and decided initiative as possible " : as saints have we not a strong and decided initiative ? Born again of the Spirit, cleansed from all sin, sanctified to do the will of God ? " Be ye transformed by the renewing of your mind," says Paul. It is because we have failed to realize that God requires intellectual vigour on the part of a saint that the devil gets his hold on the stagnant mental life of so many. To be transformed by the renewing of our mind means the courageous lifting of all our problems, individual, family, social and civic, into the spiritual domain, and habitually working out a life of practical holiness there. It is not an easy task, but a gloriously difficult one, requiring the mightiest effort of our human nature, a task which lifts us into thinking God's thoughts after Him.

" That ye may prove what is the good and acceptable and perfect will of God." God's will is only clearly understood by the development of spiritual character, consequently saints interpret the will of God differently at different times. It is not God's will that alters, but the saint's development in character. Only by intense habitual holiness, by the continual renewing of our mind, and the maintenance of an unworldly spirit, can we be assured of God's will concerning us, " even the thing which is good and acceptable and perfect." (R.V. marg.)

The Mature Christian

Ye therefore shall be perfect, as your heavenly Father is perfect. MATTHEW v. 48, R.V.

IN Matthew V verses 29–30 and verse 48 respectively our Lord refers to two things which are full of vital instruction. In vv. 29–30 He is referring to the necessity of a maimed life : "And if thy right eye offend thee, pluck it out, and cast it from thee " ; in v. 48 He refers to the life which is not maimed, but perfect. These two statements embrace the whole of our spiritual life from beginning to end.

" Ye therefore shall be perfect, as your heavenly Father is perfect." God is so almightily simple that it is impossible to complicate Him, impossible to put evil into Him or bring evil out of Him ; impossible to alter His light and His love, and the nature of the faith born in me by the Holy Ghost will take me back to the Source and enable me to see what God is like, and until I am all light and all love in Him, the things in me which are not of that character will have to pass. In the beginning of Christian experience the life is maimed because we are learning. There is the right eye to be plucked out, the right hand to be cut off, and we are apt to think that is all God means; it is not. What God means is what Jesus said, " Ye shall be perfect, as your heavenly Father is perfect." When we discern that the sword that is brought across our natural life is not for destruction, but for discipline, we get His idea exactly.

God never destroys the work of His own hands, He removes what would pervert it, that is all. Maturity is the stage where the whole life has been brought under the control of God.

1. *THE UPWARD LOOK*

Psalm cxxi portrays the upward look—" I will lift up mine eyes unto the mountains : from whence shall my help come ? My help cometh from the Lord, which made heaven and earth." The upward look of a mature Christian is not to the mountains, but to the God who made the mountains. It is the maintained set of the highest powers of a man—not star-gazing till he stumbles, but the upward gaze deliberately set towards God. He has got through the " choppy waters " of his elementary spiritual experience and now he is set on God. " I have set the Lord always before me "—but you have to fight for it.

2. *THE FORWARD LOOK*

" Thine eyes shall see the king in his beauty : they shall behold a far-stretching land " (" a land of far distances ") (Isaiah xxxiii, 17, R.V. marg.). The forward look is the look that sees everything in God's perspective whereby His wonderful distance is put on the things that are near. Caleb had the perspective of God ; the men who went up with him saw only the inhabitants of the land as giants and themselves as grasshoppers. Learn to take the long view and you will breathe the benediction of God among the squalid things that surround you. Some people never get ordinary or commonplace, they transfigure everything they touch because they have got the forward look which brings their confidence in God out into the actual details of life. The faith that does not react in the flesh is very immature. Paul was so identified with Jesus Christ that he had the audacity to say that what men saw in his life in the flesh was the very faith of the Son of God. Galatians ii, 20 is the most audacious verse in the Bible! Paul is not referring to his own elementary faith in Jesus Christ as his Saviour, but to the faith of the Son of God, and he says that that identical faith is now in him.

Fortitude in trial comes from having the long view of God. No matter how closely I am imprisoned by poverty, or tribulation, I see " the land that is very far off," and there is no drudgery on earth that is not turned Divine by the very sight. Abraham did not always have the forward look, that is why he did a scurry down to Egypt when there was a famine in the land of promise. Why shouldn't I starve for the glory of God? Immediately I fix on God's " goods," I lose the long view. If I give up to God because I want the hundredfold more, I never see God.

3. THE BACKWARD LOOK

And thine ears shall hear a word behind thee saying, This is the way, walk ye in it ; when ye turn to the right hand, and when ye turn to the left. ISAIAH xxx, 21.

The surest test of maturity is the power to look back without blinking anything. When we look back we get either hopelessly despairing or hopelessly conceited. The difference between the natural backward look and the spiritual backward look is in what we forget. Forgetting in the natural domain is the outcome of vanity—the only things I intend to remember are those in which I figure as being a very fine person! Forgetting in the spiritual domain is the gift of God. The Spirit of God never allows us to forget what we have been, but He does make us forget what we have attained to, which is quite unnatural. The surest sign that you are growing in mature appreciation of your salvation is that as you look back you never think now of the things you used to bank on before. Think of the difference between your first realisation of God's forgiveness, and your realisation of what it cost God to forgive you; the hilarity in the one case has been merged into holiness, you have become intensely devoted to God who forgave you.

Perfect Love

But whoso keepeth His word, in him verily is the love of God perfected. 1 JOHN ii, 5.

If we love one another, God dwelleth in us, and His love is perfected in us. 1 JOHN iv, 12.

1. *IN ABANDONED INDWELLING*

ROMANS v, 5.

THERE is only one Being who loves perfectly, and that is God, yet the New Testament distinctly states that we are to love as God does; so the first step is obvious. If ever we are going to have perfect love in our hearts we must have the very nature of God in us. In Romans v, 5 the Apostle Paul tells us how this is possible; he says, "the love of God is shed abroad in our hearts by the Holy Ghost which is given unto us." He is speaking not of the power to love God, but of the very love of God itself which is "shed abroad"—a superabounding word, it means that the love of God takes possession of every crook and cranny of our nature. The practical question to ask therefore is, Have I received the Holy Spirit? has it ever come to an issue with me? There is nothing on earth like the love of God when once it breaks on the soul, it may break at a midnight or a dawn, but always as a great surprise, and we begin to experience the uniting of our whole being with the nature of God. Everything in that moment becomes easy,

no command of Jesus is difficult to obey. It is not our power
to love God that enables us to obey, but the presence of the
very love of God in our heart which makes it so easy to obey
Him that we don't even know we are obeying. As you
recall to your mind the touchings of the love of God in your
life—they are always few—you will never find it impossible
to do anything He asks.

When the love of God has been shed abroad in our hearts
we have to exhibit it in the strain of life; when we are
saved and sanctified we are apt to think that there is no strain,
but Paul speaks of the " tribulation which worketh patience."
I mean by strain, not effort, but the possibility of going wrong
as well as of going right. There is always a risk, for this
reason, that God values our obedience to Him. When
God saves and sanctifies a man his personality in raised to
its highest pitch of freedom, he is free now to sin if he
wants to; before, he is not free, sin is impelling and urging
him; when he is delivered from sin he is free not to sin,
or free to sin if he chooses. The doctrine of sinless perfection and consequent freedom from temptation runs on
the line that because I am sanctified, I cannot now do wrong.
If that is so, you cease to be a man. If God put us in such
a condition that we could not disobey, our obedience would
be of no value to Him. But blessed be His Name, when by
His redemption the love of God is shed abroad in our
hearts, He gives us something to do to manifest it. Just as
human nature is put to the test in the actual circumstances
of life, so the love of God in us is put to the test. " Keep
yourselves in the love of God," says Jude, that is keep your
soul open not only to the fact that God loves you, but that
He is *in* you, in you sufficiently to manifest His perfect love
in every condition in which you can find yourself as you
rely upon Him. The curious thing is that what we are apt,
too apt, to restrain is the love of God; we have to be

careless of the expression and heed only the Source. Let our Lord be allowed to give the Holy Spirit to a man, deliver him from sin, and put His own love within him, and that man will love Him personally, passionately and devotedly. It is not an earning or a working for, but a gift and a receiving.

2. IN ABANDONED IDENTIFICATION

Love suffereth long, and is kind. 1 CORINTHIANS xiii, 4–7.
For the love of Christ constraineth us. 2 CORINTHIANS v, 14.

The Holy Ghost sheds abroad the love of God in our hearts and in 1 Corinthians xiii we see how that perfect love is to be expressed in actual life. " Love suffereth long, and is kind . . ." Substitute " the Lord " for " love," and it comes home. Jesus is the love of God Incarnate. The only exhibition of the love of God in human flesh is our Lord, and John says " as He is, even so are we in this world." God expects His love to be manifested in our redeemed lives. We make the mistake of imagining that service for others springs from love of others ; the fundamental fact is that supreme love for our Lord alone gives us the motive power of service to any extent for others —" ourselves your servants for Jesus' sake." That means I have to identify myself with God's interests in other people, and God is interested in some extraordinary people, viz., in you and in me, and He is just as interested in the person you dislike as He is in you. I don't know what your natural heart was like before God saved you, but I know what mine was like. I was misunderstood and misrepresented ; everybody else was wrong and I was right. Then when God came and gave me a spring-cleaning, dealt with my sin, and filled me with the Holy Spirit, I began to find an extraordinary alteration in myself. I still think the great marvel of the experience of salvation is not the alteration others see in you, but the alteration you find in yourself. When you come across certain people and things and remember what you used to be like in connection with them, and realise what you are now by the grace of God, you are filled with astonishment and joy; where there used to be a well of resentment and bitterness, there is now a well of sweetness.

God grant we may not only experience the indwelling of the love of God in our hearts, but go on to a hearty abandon to that love so that God can pour it out through us for His redemptive purposes for the world. He broke the life of His own Son to redeem us, and now He wants to use our lives as a sacrament to nourish others.

Sacramental Christianity

T HE word "sacramental" must be understood to mean the real presence of Christ being conveyed through the actual elements of the speech and natural life of a Christian. "Everyone therefore who shall *confess* Me before men," that is, confess with every part of me that "Jesus Christ has come in the flesh"—come, not only historically, but *in my flesh*.

1. *SACRAMENTAL SERVICE*

But far be it from me to glory, save in the cross of our Lord Jesus Christ, through whom the world hath been crucified unto me, and I unto the world. GALATIANS vi, 14, R.V. marg.

By the Cross of Christ I am saved from sin; by the Cross of Christ I am sanctified; but I never am a sacramental disciple until I deliberately lay myself on the altar of the Cross, and give myself over emphatically and entirely to be actually what I am potentially in the sight of God, viz., a member of the Body of Christ. When I swing clear of myself and my own consciousness and give myself over to Jesus Christ, He can use me as a sacrament to nourish other lives. Most of us are on the borders of consciousness, consciously serving, consciously devoted to God; it is all immature, it is not the life yet. Maturity is the life of a child —a child is never consciously childlike—so abandoned to God that the thought of being made broken bread and poured-out wine no longer unseals the fountain of tears.

When you are consciously being used as broken bread and poured-out wine you are interested in your own martyrdom, it is consciously costing you something ; when you are laid on the altar of the Cross all consciousness of self is gone, all consciousness of what you are doing for God, or of what God is doing through you, is gone. It is no longer possible to talk about " my experience of sanctification " ; you are brought to the place where you understand what is meant by our Lord's words, " Ye shall be My witnesses." Wherever a saint goes, everything he or she does becomes a sacrament in God's hands, unconsciously to himself. You never find a saint being consciously used by God ; He uses some casual thing you never thought about, which is the surest evidence that you have got beyond the stage of conscious sanctification, you are beyond all consciousness because God is taking you up into His consciousness ; you are His, and life becomes the natural simple life of a child. To be everlastingly on the look-out to do some work for God means I want to evade sacramental service—" I want to do what I want to do." Maintain the attitude of a child towards God and He will do what He likes with you. If God puts you on the shelf it is in order to season you. If He is pleased to put you in limited circumstances so that you cannot go out into the highways of service, then enter into sacramental service. Once you enter that service, you can enter no other.

2. SACRAMENTAL FELLOWSHIP

Except a corn of wheat fall into the ground and die, it abideth alone ; but if it die, it bringeth forth much fruit. JOHN xii, 24.

If you are wondering whether you are going on with God, examine yourself in the light of these words. The more

spiritually real I become, the less am I of any account,
I become more and more of the nature of a grain of wheat
falling into the earth and dying in order that it may bring
forth fruit. " He must increase, but I must decrease."
I only decrease as He increases, and He only increases
in me as I nourish His life by that which decreases me.
Am I willing to feed the life of the Son of God in me ?
If so, then He increases in me. There is no pathos in John's
words, but delight, "Would to God I could decrease more
quickly ! " If a man attracts by his personality, then his
appeal must come along the line of the particular work he
wishes to do ; but stand identified with the personality of
your Lord, like John the Baptist, and the appeal is for
His work to be done. The danger is to glory in men—
"What a wonderful personality ! " If when people get
blessed they sentimentally " moon " around me, I am to
blame because in my heart I lay the flattering unction to myself
that it is because of my way of putting things ; they begin
to idealize the one who should be being made broken bread
and poured-out wine for them. Beware of stealing souls
for whom Christ died for your own affectionate wealth.

3. SACRAMENTAL RESPONSIBILITY

*Now I rejoice in my sufferings for your sake, and fill up
on my part that which is lacking of the afflictions of Christ
in my flesh for His body's sake, which is the church.* COLOS-
SIANS i, 24.

By " sacramental responsibility " understand the solemn
determination to keep myself notably my Lord's, and to
treat as a subtle temptation of the devil the call to take on
any responsibility that conflicts with my determined identification with His interests. God's one great interest in men
is that they are redeemed ; am I identifying myself with

that interest? Notice where God puts His disapproval on human experiences, it is when we begin to adhere to our conception of what sanctification is, and forget that sanctification itself has to be sanctified. When we see Jesus we will be ashamed of our deliberately conscious experience of sanctification, that is the thing that hinders Him, because instead of other people seeing Jesus in me, they see " me " and not Jesus. We have to be sacramental elements in His hands, not only in word but in actual life. After sanctification it is difficult to state what your aim in life is, because God has taken you up into His purposes. The design for God's service is that He can use the saint as His hands or His feet. Jesus taught that spiritually we should " grow as the lilies," bringing out the life that God blesses.

His Certain Knowledge

. . . for He Himself knew what was in man. JOHN ii, 25.

OUR Lord seemed to go so easily and calmly amongst all kinds of men—when He met a man who could sink to the level of Judas He never turned cynical, never lost heart or got discouraged; and when He met a loyal loving heart like John's He was not unduly elated, He never overpraised him. When we meet extra goodness we feel amazingly hopeful about everybody, and when we meet extra badness we feel exactly the opposite; but Jesus " knew what was in man," He knew exactly what human beings were like and what they needed; and He saw in them something no one else ever saw—hope for the most degraded. Jesus had a tremendous hopefulness about man.

1. *HOW JESUS THOUGHT ABOUT MAN*

Everything Jesus Christ thought about man is summed up in the parable of the two sons (see Luke xv), viz., that man had a noble origin, that he sinned wilfully, and that he has the power to return if he will. Do we accept Jesus Christ's view, or do we make excuses for ourselves? " Oh well, I am trying my best, and I am getting a little better every day " —no one ever did! numbers of us get a little worse every day. " I didn't mean to go wrong." It was not only our great forerunner who sinned wilfully, there is a wilful element in every one of us, we sin knowing it is sin. Socrates' notion was that if you tell a man what is right, he will do it, but he neglected the big factor that a man's innermost instinct is not God. There is a potential hero in every man—and a potential skunk.

Jesus Christ's thought about man is that he is lost, and that He is the only One who can find him. " For the Son of Man came to seek and to save that which was lost." Salvation means that if a man will turn—and every man has the power to turn, if it is only a look towards the Cross, he has the power for that—if a man will but turn, he will find that Jesus is able to deliver him not only from the snare of the wrong disposition within him, but from the power of evil and wrong outside him. The words of Jesus witness to His knowledge that man has the power to turn— " Come unto Me." " Him that cometh to Me I will in no wise cast out." As soon as a man turns, God finds him. The Cross of Christ spells hope for the most despairing sinner on the face of the earth. ". . . the Son of man hath power on earth to forgive sins."

2. *HOW JESUS TREATED MEN*

Jesus Christ treated men from the standpoint of His knowledge of them, He is the supreme Master of the human heart. Recall what He said—" For from within, out of the heart of man, proceed evil thoughts . . . " consequently He was never surprised, never in a panic. When He met the rich young ruler, an upright-living, splendid young man, we read that " Jesus beholding him loved him," but He knew that at the back of all his morality was a disposition which could sin wilfully against God. " If thou wilt be perfect . . ." then come the conditions. Again,

G

when Jesus met Nicodemus, a godly man, a ruler of the synagogue, He told him he must be made all over again before he could enter the kingdom of God. Or think how Jesus treated Peter. Peter loved Jesus, he declared that he was ready to lay down his life for Him, and yet he denied Him thrice. But Jesus never lost heart over him, He had told him beforehand—". . . but I made supplication for thee, that thy faith fail not; and do thou, when once thou hast turned again, stablish thy brethren." Sin never frightened Jesus; the devil never frightened Him. Face Jesus Christ with all the power of the devil: He *was manifested, that He might destroy the works of the devil.* Are you being tripped up by the subtle power of the devil? Remember, Jesus Christ has power not only to release you, but to make you more than conqueror over all the devil's onslaughts.

" For He Himself knew what was in man "—consequently He never trusted any man, whether it was John, or Peter, or Thomas; He knew what was in them: they did not. How wonderfully the Apostle Paul learnt this lesson! Read his Epistles—" Don't glory in men, glory only in Jesus Christ and in His work in you." The Holy Spirit applies Jesus Christ's knowledge to me until I know that " in me, that is, in my flesh, dwelleth no good thing," consequently I am never dismayed at what I discover in myself, but learn to trust only what the grace of God does in me.

How does Jesus Christ treat me? Let me receive the Holy Spirit and I will very soon know. He will treat me as He treats every man—mercilessly with regard to sin. We say, " O Lord, leave a little bit of pride, a little bit of self-realization." God can never save human pride. Jesus Christ has no mercy whatever when it comes to conviction of sin. He has an amazing concern for the sinner, but no pity for sin.

3. *HOW JESUS THOUGHT ABOUT HIMSELF*

" For in that He Himself hath suffered being tempted, He is able to succour them that are tempted. He was in all points tempted like as we are, yet without sin." (Hebrews ii, 18 ; iv, 15.) These verses reveal that it was in His temptation our Lord entered into identification with our need. He took upon Him our human nature, our flesh and blood, and the Spirit drove Him into the wilderness to be tempted by the subtle power of the antagonist of God. Having " suffered being tempted " He knows how terrific are the onslaughts of the devil against human nature unaided ; He has been there, therefore He can be touched with the feeling of our infirmities. God Almighty was never " tempted in all points like as we are," Jesus Christ was. God Almighty knows all that Jesus Christ knows ; but, if I may say it reverently, *God in Christ* knows more, because *God in Christ* " suffered being tempted," and therefore He is " able to succour them that are tempted."

Those of you who have been saved by God's grace, have you accepted Jesus' thought about men and are you learning to treat them as He did ? or has your soul been rushed into a moral panic as you faced a difficult case ? If so, you have never begun to think in Christ's school. If you are rightly related to God there is no excuse for indulging in panic ; the Holy Spirit will safeguard you from alarm at immorality, and put you in the place where you can fill up that which remains behind of the afflictions of Christ. If you suffer from panic, you hinder the Holy Spirit working through you. It is easy to be shocked at immorality, but how much education in the school of Christ, how much reliance on the Holy Spirit, does it take to bring us to the place where we are shocked at pride against God? That sensitiveness is lacking to-day.

" And because iniquity shall abound, the love of many shall wax cold." The portrait of many of us was sketched in these words of Jesus. Think of the worst man you know, not the worst man you can think of, because that is vague, have you any hope for him ? Does the Holy Spirit begin to convey to your mind the wonder of that man being presented perfect in Christ Jesus ? That is the test as to whether you have been learning to think about men as Jesus thought of them. The Holy Spirit brings us into sympathy with the work Jesus has done on behalf of men in that He is " able to save to the uttermost them that come unto God by Him."

How the Apostle Paul Returns Thanks

But I have received all, and abound : I am full, having received of Epaphroditus the things which were sent from you, an odour of a sweet smell, a sacrifice acceptable, well pleasing to God. PHIL. iv, 18.

THE Apostle Paul refused to take money-help from any of the Churches he founded and over which he watched so carefully, and his reasons for this are expounded in 1 Corinthians ix (see also a significant reference in Acts xx, 34), the one exception being the Church at Philippi. Paul's imprisonment had revived their affectionate interest, and he writes to thank them for a further gift through Epaphroditus, as, " even in Thessalonica ye sent once and again unto my necessity." The Epistle is a letter of gratitude for these gifts, and along with his thanks Paul combines solicitations and teaching, and deals with some of the grandest, most fundamental truths, e.g., Chapter II.

The letter is addressed to " all the saints in Christ Jesus which are at Philippi " from " Paul and Timothy, servants of Jesus Christ." This is a wonderfully courteous touch, Paul does not call himself here " an apostle of Jesus Christ," but by a name that embraces Timothy, because he was with him when the Church was founded—" bond-servants of Christ Jesus."

CHAPTER I

But I would ye should understand, brethren, that the things which happened unto me have fallen out rather unto the furtherance of the gospel. v. 12.

The fortune of misfortune ! That is Paul's way of looking at his captivity. He does not want them to be depressed on his account, or to imagine that God's purpose has been hindered ; he says it has not been hindered, but furthered. The very things that looked so disastrous have turned out to be the most opportune, so that on this account his heart bounds with joy, and the note of rejoicing comes out through the whole Letter.

Some indeed preach Christ even of envy and strife ; and some also of good will. v. 15-18.

Paul was severity itself in dealing with those in Galatia who proclaimed the Gospel from the wrong motive (see Gal. i, 7-8; ii, 4-5; v, 7-12) ; here, he deals with the matter more gently, what is the reason for the difference ? In the first case false brethren had insinuated themselves into the Church with the set purpose of unsettling the believers and bringing them into bondage ; in this case the motive, he says, was " to raise up affliction for me in my bonds." Whenever harm is being done to the flock of God it must be tracked out and dealt with rigorously ; personal injury is another matter. " Whosoever shall smite thee on thy right cheek, turn to him the other also," said our Lord, and Paul exhibits that spirit when he says, " What then ? not withstanding, every way, whether in pretence, or in truth, Christ is preached ; and I therein do rejoice, yea, and will rejoice."

This brings us up against a big problem, a problem our Lord refers to in Matthew vii, 21-23. Because God honours

His word no matter how preached or by whom, we naturally infer that if His word is blessed, souls saved, demons cast out, mighty works done, surely the preacher must be a servant of God. It does not follow by any means. An instrument of God and a servant of God ought to be identical, but our Lord's words and Paul's are instances where they are not. It does not impair the inspiration of the Gospel to have it preached by a bad man, but the influence of the preacher, worthy or unworthy, apart altogether from his preaching, has a tremendous effect. If I know a man to be a bad man the sinister influence of his personality neutralises altogether the effect of God's message through him to me ; but let me be quite sure that my intuition springs from my relationship to God and not from human suspicion.

CHAPTER II

Fulfil ye my joy, that ye be like-minded, having the same love, being of one accord, of one mind. v. 2.

In verses 1–4 Paul is arguing—" If you are rightly related to God in Christ, the life of the Son of God in you makes you identical with Him, so that the same ' comfort of love,' the same fellowship of the Spirit, the same ' mercies ' that marked Him, mark you." How we water down the amazing revelation made in the New Testament, that we are made one with Christ ! " I live ; yet not I, but Christ liveth in me."

Let this mind be in you, which was also in Christ Jesus. v. 5.

We are not given a fully formed reasoning Christian mind when we are born again, we are given the Spirit of Jesus, but not His mind, we have to form that. The " mind " Paul urges the Philippian Christians to form is not the mind of Almighty God, but the mind of Christ Jesus, " who, being in the form of God, thought it not robbery to be equal with God " (" not a thing to be grasped," R.V. marg.). This was the central citadel of the temptation—" You are the Son of God, assert your prerogative ; You will bring the world to Your feet if You will remember who You are and use Your power." The answer Jesus made was, " I did not come to do My own will, although I am the Son of God, I am here in this order of things for one purpose only, to do the will of My Father." When we are sanctified the same temptation comes to us—" You are a child of God, identified with Jesus, presume on it, think it something to be grasped, to be proud of." We are saved and sanctified for one purpose, that God's will might be done in us as it was in our Lord.

. . . work out your own salvation with fear and trembling. For it is God which worketh in you both to will and to do of His good pleasure. v. 12–13.

These verses combine all we understand by the great efficacious work of grace of God in salvation and sanctification. " You are saved," says Paul, " now *work it out* : be consistent in character with what God has worked in." The only estimate of consistent Christian character is the life of Jesus being made manifest in our mortal flesh. People talk a lot about their " experience " of sanctification and too often there is nothing in it, it doesn't work out in the bodily life or in the mind, it is simply a doctrine ; with Paul it was the mainspring of his life. " For it is God which worketh in you *to will* . . . " It is nonsense to talk about a man's free will, a man's will is only fundamentally free in God, that is, he is only free when the law of God and the Spirit of God are actively working in his will by his own choice.

. . . that ye may be blameless and harmless, the sons of God without rebuke, in the midst of a crooked and perverse nation, among whom ye shine as lights in the world. v. 15 marg.

—that means on this earth, not in heaven. We have to shine as lights in the squalid places of earth ; we can't shine in heaven, our light would be put out in two seconds. " That ye may be blameless "—if ever we are to be blameless, undeserving of censure in the sight of God who sees down to the motive of our motives, it must be by the supernatural power of God. The meaning of the Cross is just that—I can not only have the marvellous work of God's grace done in my heart, but can have the proof of it in my life. " The Higher Christian Life " phraseology is apt to be nothing in the world but the expression of a futile and sorrowful struggle, adoring God for what we are in His Divine anticipation but never can be in actuality. It is only when I realise that God's anticipations for me are presented as participations through the power of the Holy Spirit, that I become that peculiarly humble person, a disciple of the Lord Jesus.

Yea, and if I am poured out as a drink-offering upon the sacrifice and service of your faith, I joy, and rejoice with you all. v. 17 R.V. marg.

Paul's conception of the altar of sacrifice is " spending and being spent " for the sake of the elementary children of God. He has no other end and aim than that—to be broken bread and poured-out wine in the hands of God that others might be nourished and fed. (Cf. Colossians i, 24.) The great Saviour and His great apostle go hand-in-hand : the Son of God sacrificed Himself to redeem men ; Paul, His bondservant, sacrificed himself that men might come to know they are redeemed, that they have been bought with a price and are not their own ; it was no false note when Paul said, *Christ liveth in me.*

CHAPTER III

. . . as touching the law, a Pharisee. v. 5.

Saul of Tarsus did easily what all other Pharisees did, but his conscience would not allow him to be a hypocrite easily. His ardent nature tried to make his inner life come up to the standard of the law, and the tragedy of his failure is portrayed in Romans vii. No one was ever so introspective, so painfully conscious of weakness and inability to keep the law, as Paul, so when he says, " Christ is the end of the law unto righteousness " he is making an intensely practical statement. He is stating the fact that Jesus Christ has planted in him as a sheer gift of God's grace the life that enables him now to fulfil all the law of God—" not having mine own righteousness, which is of the law, but that which is through the faith of Christ, the righteousness which is of God by faith : " " Imputed " means *imparted* with Paul.

If any other man thinketh that he hath whereof he might trust in the flesh, I more. v. 4.

In verses 4–6 Paul catalogues the things that used to be " gains " to him, the things which were a recommendation to him in the eyes of the world (cf. Galatians i, 13–14) ; but, he says, " I fling them all overboard as refuse, that I may win Christ." The whole of Paul's life has been re-determined by regeneration, and he estimates now from an entirely different standard. The things from which we have to loose ourselves are the good things of the old creation as well as the bad, e.g., our natural virtues, because our

natural virtues can never come anywhere near what Jesus
Christ wants.

*That I may know Him, and the power of His resurrection,
and the fellowship of His sufferings . . .* v. 10.

Paul talks more about suffering than any of the apostles,
but any suffering that is less than " fellowship with His
sufferings " he treats very lightly—" our light affliction . . .";
" sufferings not worthy to be compared with the glory."
Jesus suffered " according to the will of God," and to be
made a partaker of His sufferings destroys every element of
self-pity, of self-interest, of self-anything.

. . . not as though I were already perfect. v. 12.

Let us therefore, as many as be perfect . . . v. 15.

Nothing but wilful perversion would make anyone mis-
understand these two " perfections."   In v. 12 Paul is
speaking of the perfection of consummation not attainable
in this life ; in v. 15 he speaks of a perfection of fitness
demanded now.   " Remember, though you are perfectly
adjusted to God, you have attained to nothing yet."   The
idea is that of a Marathon runner, practising and practising
until he is perfectly fit ; when he is perfectly fit he hasn't
begun the race, he is only perfectly fit to begin.   By regeneration we are put into perfect relationship to God, then we
have the same human nature, working along the same lines,
but with a different mainspring.   " Not that I am already
made perfect " : that is the perfection of consummation ;
" I haven't got there yet," says Paul; " but I follow after,
if so be that I may apprehend that for which also I was
apprehended by Christ Jesus."   Paul was absolutely Christ-
centred, he had lost all interest in himself in an absorbing
passionate interest in Christ.   Very few saints get where he
got, and we are to blame for not getting there.   We thank

God for saving and sanctifying us and continually revert to
these experiences : Paul reverted to one thing only—" When
it pleased God . . . to reveal His Son in me," then he never
bothered any more about himself. We try to efface ourselves
by an effort ; Paul did not efface himself by an effort, his
interest in himself simply died right out when he became
identified with the death of Jesus.

*For many walk, of whom I have told you often, and now
tell you even weeping, that they are the enemies of the cross
of Christ.*" v. 18.

Why did Paul say "enemies of *the cross of Christ*", and not
" enemies of *Christ* "? The test all through is true-ness to
the Cross. What the enemies of the cross so strenuously
oppose is identification on the part of the believer with what
the death of Christ on the Cross represents, viz., death to
sin in every shape and form. Look at the tremendous words
Paul uses, they express the agony of his heart over those who
are the enemies of that moral identification. Their god is
" themselves "—what develops " me " ; not that which
takes " me " right out of the road and gives the Son of God
a chance to manifest Himself in me. What was it God
condemned in the Cross ? Self-realisation. Have I come
to a moral agreement with God about that ? To say that what
God condemned in the Cross was social sins is not true ;
what God condemns in the Cross is *sin,* which is away
further down than any moral quirks.

CHAPTER IV

*Therefore, my brethren, dearly beloved and longed for,
my joy and crown, so stand fast in the Lord, my dearly
beloved.* v. I.

Notice Paul's earnest solicitation over those who have

been saved through his ministry; he carried every convert on his heart to the end of his life, or of theirs.

Be careful for nothing. v. 6.

The enemy of saintliness is carefulness over the wrong thing. The culture of the Christian life is to learn to be carefully careless over everything saving our relationship to God. It is not sin that keeps us from going on spiritually, but " the cares of the world," " the lusts of other things " that crowd out any consideration of God. We reverse the teaching of Jesus, we don't seek first the Kingdom of God, we seek every other thing first, and the result accords with what Jesus said, the word He puts in is choked and becomes unfruitful.

Finally, brethren, whatsoever things are true . . . take account of these things. v. 8 R.V. marg.

" Glean your thinking "—one of the hardest things to do. For instance, it is essentially difficult to think along the lines laid down in 1 Corinthians xiii: " Love . . . taketh not account of evil " ; apart from God we do take account of evil, we reason from that standpoint. The majority of us are not spiritual thinkers, but once we begin to think on the basis of our relationship to God through the Redemption, we find it a most revolutionary thing. We are not saved by thinking, we form our nous, a responsible intelligence, by thinking, and immediately we face the application of the Redemption to the details of our lives, we find it means everything has to be readjusted bit by bit.

Problemata Mundi

Hast thou considered My servant Job, that there is none like him in the earth, a perfect and an upright man, one that feareth God, and escheweth evil? JOB. i, 8.

THE Book of Job mirrors for all time the problem of things as they have been, as they are, and as they will be until they are altered by the manifestation of a new heaven and a new earth. When things go well a man does not want God, but when things get difficult and suffering begins to touch him, he finds the problem of the world inside his own skin. The slander of men is against God when disasters occur. If you have never felt inclined to call God cruel and hard, it is a question whether you have ever faced any problems at all. Job's utterances are those of a man who suffers without any inkling as to why he suffers; yet he discerns intuitively that what is happening to him is not in God's order, although it is in His permissive will. All through, Job stands for two things: that God is just, and that he is relatively innocent. Remember, Job was never told the preface to his own story; he did not know that he had been chosen to be the battleground between God and Satan. Satan's contention was that no man loved God for His own sake—" Doth Job serve God for nought?" " Job only loves You because You bless him, let me curse his blessings and I will prove it to You." Satan's primary concern is to sneer against God, he is after disconcerting God, putting God in a corner, so to speak, where He will have to take action along Satan's proposed lines.

There are circumstances in life which make us know that Satan's sneer is pretty near the mark. I love God as long as He blesses me, saves my soul and puts me right for heaven; but supposing He should see fit to let the worst things happen to me, would I say, " Go on, do it " and love Him still? The point is that God's honour is at stake in a man who suffers as did this " perfect and upright " man. Part of the problem was that in the bargain Satan made with God, he implied that God must keep out of sight; and God did, He never once showed Himself to Job. The presentation of the controversy between God and Satan is such that Satan has everything on his side and God nothing on His, so much so that God dare not say a word to Job till he had proved himself worthy. Job cannot answer one of the charges the friends bring against him, he tears their arguments to shreds in the fervour of his pain, yet he clings to it, " I will believe God, in spite of everything that seems to be contradicting His character."

The Apostle James talks about " the patience of Job "— Job patient! He was patient, but only to God. There is nothing logical about Job, his statements are wild and chaotic, but underneath there is an implicit understanding of God's character. He is sure of God even though He seems to be doing everything to ruin him, and he draws steadily nearer God as his friends withdraw themselves from him, heaping their anathemas upon him. They slander Job while standing up for God; but in the end God says, " Ye have not spoken of Me the thing that is right, as My servant Job hath." The citadel of true religion is personal relationship to God, let come what will.

Where does our mind rest regarding suffering? The Bible makes little of physical suffering. The modern mind looks on suffering and pain as an unmitigated curse; the Bible puts something akin to purifying in connection with suffering, e.g., " for he that hath suffered in the flesh hath ceased from sin " (1 Peter iv, 1). The thing that moves us is the pathos arising from physical suffering ; the anguish of a soul trying to find God we put down to lunacy. The only way traditional belief can be transformed into a personal possession is by suffering. Look at what you say you believe, not an atom of it is yours saving the bit you have proved by suffering and in no other way.

Never run away with the idea that Satan is sceptical of all virtue, he knows God too well and human nature too well to have such a shallow scepticism ; he is sceptical only of virtue that has not been tried. Faith un-tried is simply a promise and a possibility, which we may cause to fail ; tried faith is the pure gold. Faith must be tried, otherwise it is of no worth to God. Think of the dignity it gives to a man's life to know that God has put His honour in his keeping. Our lives mean more than we can tell, they mean that we are fulfilling some purpose of God about which we know nothing any more than Job did. God's government of the world is not for material prosperity, but for moral ends, for the production of moral characters, in the sense of holy characters. Time is nothing to God.

" . . . the Lord gave Job twice as much as he had before. . . . So the Lord blessed the latter end of Job more than his beginning " (Chapter xlii, 10–12). The charge is made that because God gave Job back his material prosperity, therefore the whole argument of the Book falls to the ground ; but the blessing of God on Job was nothing more than an outward manifestation accompanying the certainty he now possessed, viz., that he loves God and that God loves him. It is the overflowing favour of God poured out on a loved son who has come through the ordeal and won his way straight through to God.

A Fatal Error of
Indignant Integrity

And he was angry, and would not go in. LUKE xv, 28.

WE get the idea that wrong views of God and of goodness arise from a life that is wrong; the Bible shows that wrong views of God and of goodness may arise out of a life that is right. The parable of the two sons is an example of this. The younger brother was a wastrel; the elder brother was a man of integrity, there was not a spot on his character—" neither transgressed I at any time thy commandment." Everything that led him to take up the position he did was perfectly justifiable, it was the protest of an upright man, but he made the fatal error of misinterpreting his father's ways and refusing to enter into a love that was too big for this earth. Many good upright people misinterpret God's ways because they do not take into account first of all the matter of personal relationship to God. They say because we are the creatures of God, we are the sons and daughters of God; Jesus Christ taught with profound insistence that we are sons and daughters of God only by an inner disposition, the disposition of love, which works implicitly. The Bible states that " love is of God." The difficulty arises out of our individuality, which is hard and tight, segregated from others; personality is never isolated, it always merges, and is characterised by an implicit understanding of things. The attitude of the elder brother is individual entirely, he is merged into nothing of the nature of love, consequently he misunderstands his father and demands that his ways ought to be more clearly justifiable to human reason. God's ways never are, because the basis of things fundamentally is not reasonable ; if it were, God would be cruel to allow what He does. Our reason is simply an instrument, the way we explain things, it is not the basis of things. The problems of life are only explainable by means of a right relationship to God. If we ask for a reasonable explanation of God's ways in Providence, such as are stated in the Book of Job, or of the puzzles of Nature referred to by Paul in Romans viii, 19–23, we will end in misinterpreting God ; but when we receive the disposition Jesus Christ came to give us, we find our problems are explained implicitly. There is no such thing as sin to common-sense reasoning, therefore no meaning in the Cross because that view rules out what the Bible bases everything on, viz., the hiatus between God and man produced by sin, and the Cross where sin is dealt with. When common-sense reasoning comes to the Cross it is embarrassed, it looks at the death of Jesus as the death of a martyr, One who lived beyond His dispensation. According to the New Testament, the Cross is the Cross of God, not of a man. The problems of Providence, the puzzles of Nature, the paradoxes of Christianity do not bother everybody, they are the problems of men who are good and upright, but distinctly individual, and their individuality causes them to misinterpret God's ways and repudiate Christianity.

" . . . as soon as this thy son was come, which hath devoured thy living with harlots, thou hast killed for him the fatted calf." The elder brother is right, not wrong, according to all reasonable human standards, when he says of the prodigal, " Such a character ought not to be allowed in the home, he ought to be excluded." A bad man would have said " Oh well, it doesn't matter, he has made mistakes, we all do." Embarrassment always arises in the domain to ethics when we make the basis of Christianity adherence of principles instead of personal relationship to God. What is called Christianity, our charity and benevolence, is not Christianity as the New Testament teaches it, it is simply adherence to certain principles. Jesus tells us to " give to him that asketh thee "—not because he deserves it, or because he needs it, but " because I tell you to." Ask yourself, " Do I deserve all I have got ? " The teaching of Jesus revolutionizes our modern conception of charity.

A false idea of God's honour ends in misinterpreting His ways. It is the orthodox type of Christian who by sticking to a crude idea of God's character, presents the teaching which says, " God loves you when you are good, but not when you are bad." God loves us whether we are good or bad. That is the marvel of His love. " For I came not to call the righteous, but sinners to repentance "—whether there are any righteous is open to question. " The righteous have no need of Me ; I came for the sinful, the ungodly, the weak." If I am not sinful and ungodly and weak, I don't need Him at all.

The presentation Jesus gives of the father is that he makes no conditions when the prodigal returns, neither does he bring home to him any remembrance of the far country—the elder brother does that. It is the revelation of the unfathomable, unalterable, amazing love of God. We would feel much happier in our backslidden condition if only we knew it had altered God towards us, but we know that immediately we do come back we will find Him the same, and this is one of the things that keeps men from coming back. If God would only be angry and demand an apology, it would be a gratification to our pride. When we have done wrong we like to be lashed for it. God never lashes. Jesus does not represent the father as saying, " You have been so wicked that I cannot take you back as my son, I will make you a servant " ; but as saying,

Bring forth quickly the best robe and put it on him ; and put a ring on his hand, and shoes on his feet ; and bring the fatted calf, and kill it, and let us eat, and make merry : for this my son was dead, and is alive again ; he was lost, and is found.

Divine Paradox

THERE is probably no more prominent feature in Bible revelation than that of paradox. In Revelation V the apostle John records that in his vision he was told "the Lion of the tribe of Juda, hath prevailed to open the book"—and he says, "lo, in the midst of the throne stood a Lamb"! We find a paradox of a similar nature in the Book of Isaiah. The prophet has been looking for some great conquering army of the Lord, and instead he sees a lonely Figure, "travelling in the greatness of his strength." If you take all the manifestations of God in the Old Testament you find them a mass of contradictions : now God is pictured as a Man, now as a Woman, now as a lonely Hero, now as a suffering Servant, and until we come to the revelation in the New Testament these conflicting characteristics but add confusion to our conception of God. But immediately we see Jesus Christ, we find all the apparent contradictions blended in one unique Person.

Drummond in his *Natural Law in the Spiritual World*, surely makes a fundamental blunder by that very statement, and surely the contention in Butler's *Analogy* is right—that as there is a law in the natural world so there is also a law in the spiritual world, but that they are not the same laws, the one is the complement of the other. Unless this is borne in mind by the student of Scripture, and he learns to rely on the Holy Spirit to interpret the spiritual law as he relies on his own spirit to interpret the natural law, he will not only end in confusion, but will be in danger of disparaging the spiritual law in the Bible universe in favour of the natural law in the common-sense universe.

And I saw in the right hand of him that sat on the throne a book . . . sealed with seven seals. v. i.

I am considering the Book in one aspect only, viz., as containing a knowledge of the future, an understanding of the Providence of God in the present, together with a grasp of the past. The deepest clamour of a man's nature once he is awake is to know the "whence" and "whither" of life—"Whence came I?" "Why am I here?" "Where am I going?" In all ages men have tried to pry into the secrets of the future, astrologers, necromancers, spiritualists, or whatever name you may call them by, have all tried to open the Book, but without success, because it is a sealed Book. "I wept much," says John, "because no one was found worthy to open the book, or to look thereon."

Because of the sealed character of the Book men become indifferent and cease to be exercised over the "whence" and "whither" of human destiny; they take no interest in Bible revelation, and are amused at our earnest solicitation on their behalf—"It is all about something we cannot know, and there is no one who can tell us." Others say, "There is nothing to know"; not, "We cannot know," but "There is nothing to know, a man lives his life, then dies, and that is all there is." The Psalmist refers to such men when he says, "The fool hath said in his heart, There is no God." There are others whose sensitive spirit gives them an implicit sense that there is more than this life; there are hidden deeps in their heart that human life and its friendships can never satisfy. The scenes of earth, its sunsets and sunrises, its "huge and thoughtful nights" all awaken an elemental sadness which makes them wonder why they were born, and they feel keenly because the Book is sealed and there is no one able to open it.

But would to God all men knew that there *is* Someone who is worthy to open the Book !

And one of the elders said unto me, Weep not : behold the Lion of the tribe of Juda, the Root of David, hath prevailed to open the book, and to loose the seven seals thereof. v. 5.

Who is this Worthy One ? If one may say it with reverence, realizing the limitation of language, God Himself had to be proved Worthy to open the Book. In the Person of Jesus Christ God became Man, He trod this earth with naked feet,

> *and wrought*
> *With human hands the creed of creeds*
> *In loveliness and perfect deeds.*

By His holy life, by His moral integrity and supreme spiritual greatness, Jesus Christ proved that He was worthy to open the Book. The Book can be opened by only one Hand, the pierced hand of the Worthy One, our Saviour Jesus Christ.

The childish idea that because God is great He can do anything, good or bad, right or wrong, and we must say nothing, is erroneous. The meaning of moral worth is that certain things are impossible to it : " it is impossible for God to lie " ; it is impossible for Jesus Christ to contradict His own holiness or to become other than He is. The profound truth for us is that Jesus Christ is the Worthy One not because He was God Incarnate, but because He was God Incarnate on the human plane. " Being made in the likeness of men " He accepted our limitations and lived on this earth a life of perfect holiness. Napoleon said of Jesus Christ that He had succeeded in making of every

human soul an appendage of His own—why ? Because He
had the genius of holiness. There have been great military
geniuses, intellectual giants, geniuses of statesmen, but
these only exercise influence over a limited number of
men ; Jesus Christ exercises unlimited sway over all men
because He is the altogether Worthy One.

*And I beheld, and, lo, in the midst of the throne . . .
stood a Lamb as it had been slain.* v. 6.

Jesus Christ is the supreme Sacrifice for the sin of the
world ; He is " the Lamb of God, which taketh away the
sin of the world ! " How the Death of Jesus looms all through
the Bible ! It is through His death that we are made partakers
of His life and can have gifted to us a pure heart, which He
says is the condition for seeing God.

" Having . . . seven eyes," The Lamb is not only the
supreme Sacrifice for man's sin, He is the Searcher of
hearts, searching to the inmost recesses of mind and motive.
It is not a curious searching, not an uncanny searching,
but the deep wholesome searching the Holy Spirit gives
in order to convict men of their sin and need of a Saviour ;
then when they come to the Cross, and through it accept
deliverance from sin, Jesus Christ becomes the Sovereign
of their lives, they love Him personally and passionately
beyond all other loves of earth.

*And He came and took the book out of the right hand of
him that sat upon the throne.* v. 7.

Jesus Christ and He alone is able to satisfy the craving
of the human heart to know the " whence " and " whither "
of life. He enables men to understand that they have come
into this life from a deep purpose in the heart of God ;
that the one thing they are here for is to get readjusted to
God and become His lovers. And whither are we going ?

We are going to where the Book of Life is opened, and we enter into an effulgence of glory we can only conceive of now at rare moments.

In the days of His flesh Jesus Christ exhibited this Divine paradox of the Lion and the Lamb. He was the Lion in majesty, rebuking the winds and demons: He was the Lamb in meekness, "who when He was reviled, reviled not again." He was the Lion in power, raising the dead: He was the Lamb in patience—who was "brought as a lamb to the slaughter, and as a sheep before her shearers is dumb, so He openeth not His mouth." He was the Lion in authority, "Ye have heard that it hath been said . . . *but I say unto you* . . .": He was the Lamb in gentleness, "Suffer the little children to come unto Me . . . and He took them up in His arms, put His hand upon them and blessed them."

In our personal lives Jesus Christ proves Himself to be all this—He is the Lamb to expiate our sins, to lift us out of condemnation and plant within us His own heredity of holiness: He is the Lion to rule over us, so that we gladly say, "the government of this life shall be upon His shoulders." And what is true in individual life is to be true also in the universe at large. The time is coming when the Lion of the Tribe of Judah shall reign, and when "the kingdoms of this world shall become the kingdoms of our Lord, and of His Christ."

One remaining paradox—In Revelation vi, 16 "the wrath of the Lamb" is mentioned. We know what the wrath of a lion is like—but *the wrath of the Lamb !*—it is beyond our conception. All one can say about it is that the wrath of God is the terrible obverse side of the love of God.

Memory of Sin in the Saint

. . . for that He counted me faithful, putting me into the ministry; who was before a blasphemer, and a persecutor, and injurious. 1 TIMOTHY i, 13.

. . . and such were some of you. 1 CORINTHIANS vi, 11.

NO aspect of Christian life and service is in more need of revision than our attitude to the memory of sin in the saint. When the Apostle Paul said "forgetting those things which are behind," he was talking not about sin, but about his spiritual attainment. Paul never forgot what he had been; it comes out repeatedly in the Epistles —"For I am the least of the apostles, that am not meet to be called an apostle" (1 Corinthians xv, 9); "unto me who am less than the least of all saints, is this grace given" (Ephesians iii, 8); ". . . sinners, of whom I am chief" (1 Timothy i, 15). And these are the utterances of a ripe, glorious servant of God.

If one wants a touchstone for the depth of true spiritual Christianity, one will surely find it in this matter of the memory of sin. There are those who exhibit a Pharisaic holiness, they thank God with an arrogant offensiveness that they are "not as other men are"; they have forgotten the horrible pit and miry clay from whence they were taken, and their feet set upon a rock through the might of the

Atonement. Perhaps the reason they condemn others who have fallen and been restored is the old human failing of making a virtue out of necessity. Their lives have been shielded, the providence of God has never allowed them to be enmeshed in the subtle snares other men have encountered and whose fall has plunged them into an agony of remorse. May the conviction of God come with swift and stern rebuke upon any one who is remembering the past of another, and deliberately choosing to forget his restoration through God's grace. When a servant of God meets these sins in others, let him be reverent with what he does not understand and leave God to deal with them.

Certain forms of sin shock us far more than they shock God. The sin that shocks God, the sin that broke His heart on Calvary, is not the sin that shocks us. The sin that shocks God is the thing which is highly esteemed among men—self-realization, pride, my right to myself. We have no right to have the attitude to any man or woman as if he or she had sunk to a lower level than those of us who have never been tempted on the line they have. The conventions of society and our social relationships make it necessary for us to take this attitude, but we have to remember that in the sight of God there are no social conventions, and that external sins are no whit worse in His sight than the pride which hates the rule of the Holy Ghost while the life is morally clean. May God have mercy on any one of us who forgets this, and allows spiritual pride or superiority and a sense of his own unsulliedness, to put a barrier between him and those whom God has lifted from depths of sin he cannot understand.

Holiness is the only sign that a man is repentant in the New Testament sense, and a holy man is not one who has his eyes set on his own whiteness, but one who is personally and passionately devoted to the Lord who saved him—

one whom the Holy Ghost takes care shall never forget that God has made him what he is by sheer sovereign grace. Accept as the tender touch of God, not as a snare of the devil, every memory of sin the Holy Ghost brings home to you, keeping you in the place where you remember what you once were and what you now are by His grace.

" This is a faithful saying, and worthy of all acceptation, that Christ Jesus came into the world to save sinners ; of whom I am chief." (1 Timothy i, 15.)—*sinners, of whom I am chief*. What a marvellous humility it betokens for a man to say that and mean it ! In the early days of the sterner form of Calvinism a man's belief about God and about his own destiny frequently produced a wistful, self-effacing humility ; but the humility Paul manifests was produced in him by the remembrance that Jesus, whom he had scorned and despised, whose followers he had persecuted, whose Church he had harried, not only had forgiven him, but made him His chief apostle : *Unto me, who am less than the least of all the saints, is this grace given, that I should preach among the Gentiles the unsearchable riches of Christ.*

" Howbeit for this cause I obtained mercy, that in me first Jesus Christ might shew forth all longsuffering, for a pattern to them which should hereafter believe on Him to life everlasting." Here is the true attitude of the servant of God—" since God has done this for me, I can despair of no man on the face of the earth." Show such a servant of God the backslider, the sinner steeped in the iniquity of our cities, and there will spring up in his heart an amazing well of compassion and love for that one, because he has himself experienced the grace of God which goes to the uttermost depths of sin and lifts to the highest heights of salvation.

But where sin abounded, grace did abound more exceedingly.

Celebration or Surrender?

WE begin our Christian life by believing what we are
told to believe, then we have to go on to so assimilate
our beliefs that they work out in a way that redounds
to the glory of God. The danger is in multiplying the acceptation of beliefs we do not make our own. Every now and
again we find ourselves lost in wonder at the marvel of the
Redemption; it is a wholesome initial stage, but if it is
made the final stage it is perilous. The difficulty of believing
in the Redemption in the sense of assimilating it is that it
demands renunciation. I have to give up my right to myself
in complete surrender to my Lord before what I celebrate
becomes a reality. There is always the danger of celebrating
what Jesus Christ has done and forgetting the need on our
part of moral surrender to Him; if we evade the surrender
we become the more intense in celebrating what He has
done.

1. THE SNARE OF EMOTIONAL RAPTURE

*And Peter answered and said to Jesus, Master, it is good
for us to be here. Mark ix, 2–8.*

Be quick to notice how God brings you rapidly from
emotional rapture into contact with the sordid commonplace
actualities of life. There are times in the Providence of
God when He leads us apart by ourselves, when Jesus
reveals Himself to us and we see Him transfigured. The

place " apart by ourselves " may be a prayer meeting, a service, a talk with a friend, a sunrise or a sunset, when we are stirred to the depths and see what we are unable to utter ; the snare is to imagine that that is all God means ; He means much more. " And there was a cloud overshadowed them : and a voice come out of that cloud, saying, This is my beloved Son : hear Him "—not, " This is My beloved Son : now spend halcyon days with Him on the Mount." Beware of celestial sensuality. No matter what your experience, you may be trapped by sensuality any time. Sensuality is not sin, it is the way the body works in connection with circumstances whereby I begin to satisfy myself. Mary Magdalene was in danger of making this blunder, but Jesus said, " Touch Me not "—" Don't try and hold Me by your senses, but go and do what I say." Always the thrust out into the actual, because it is there you exhibit whether your emotional rapture has seduced you, made you unfit for actualities.

After a time of rapt contemplation when your mind has been absorbing the truth of God, watch the kind of people God will bring round you, not people dressed in the " cast-off nimbus " of some saint, but ordinary commonplace people just like yourself. We imagine that God must engineer special circumstances for us, peculiar sufferings ; He never does, because that would feed our pride ; He engineers things which from the standpoint of human pride are a humiliation.

" And suddenly when they had looked round about, they saw no man any more, save Jesus only with themselves." (v. 8.) Instead of its being, " no cross, no crown," spiritually, it is " no crown, no cross." We are crowned by the moment of rapture, but that is not the end, it is the beginning of being brought down into the demon-possessed valley to bear the cross for Him there. With a sudden rush we find no Moses, no Elijah, no transfiguration-glory, and we fear as we enter the cloud, till we come to the place where there is " no man, save Jesus only." As men and women we have to live in this world, in its misery and sinfulness, and we must do the same if we are disciples. Of all people we should be able to go down into the demon-possessed valley, because once we have seen Jesus transfigured it is impossible to lose heart or be discouraged.

2. *THE SINCERITY OF EXPERIMENTAL REALIZATION*

Yea doubtless, and I count all things but loss for the excellency of the knowledge of Christ Jesus my Lord. . . PHIL. 3, 8.

Paul goes on to state that he not only *estimated* the cost, he experienced it—" for whom I have suffered the loss of all things," that I may win Christ and be found in Him, not having mine own righteousness. . . . " Imagine anyone who has seen Jesus Christ transfigured saying he is sorry to find himself mean and ignoble ! The more I whine about being a miserable sinner, the more I am hurting the Holy Spirit. It simply means I don't agree with God's judgment of me, I think after all I am rather desirable : God thought me so undesirable that He sent His Son to save me. To discover I am what God says I am ought to make me glad ; if I am glad over anything I discover in myself, I am very short-sighted. The only point of rest is in the Lord Himself.

Since mine eyes have looked on Jesus,
I've lost sight of all beside . . .
So enchained my spirit's vision
Gazing on the Crucified.

BOOKS BY OSWALD CHAMBERS

	net s. d.	post free s. d.
My Utmost for His Highest	9 6	10 0
The Place of Help (*Devotional Readings*)		
Conformed to His Image		
God's Workmanship	7 6	7 10
The Psychology of Redemption	*each*	
So Send I You (*Missionary Studies*)		
Biblical Psychology		
Outline Studies on "Biblical Psychology"	9	11
Studies in the Sermon on the Mount	6 0	6 4
Baffled to Fight Better (*Book of Job*)		
He Shall Glorify Me	5 6	5 10
Shade of His Hand (*Book of Ecclesiastes*)		
Not Knowing Whither (*The Life of Abraham*)	5 0	5 4
If Thou wilt be Perfect	*each*	
Disciples Indeed		
Biblical Ethics	4 6	4 10
If Ye shall Ask	*each*	
The Moral Foundations of Life	4 0	4 4
The Philosophy of Sin	*each*	
The Shadow of an Agony		
Approved unto God	3 6	3 10
Workmen of God (*The Cure of Souls*)	*each*	
Bringing Sons unto Glory		
(*Studies in the Life of Our Lord*)	3 0	3 3
Facing Reality	*each*	
A Little Book of Prayers	2 6	2 9
As He Walked (*Christian Experience*)		
Grow up into Him (*Christian Habits*)		
Our Brilliant Heritage (*Sanctification*)		
Thy Great Redemption	1 6	1 8
The Highest Good	*each*	
The Pilgrim's Song Book		
Talks on the Soul of a Christian		
Called of God		
The Ministry of the Unnoticed	1 3	1 5
The Fighting Chance	*each*	
The Making of a Christian	1 0	1 2
The Patience of the Saints	*each*	
The Discipline Series :		
(1) Divine Guidance, *64 pp.*	1 6	1 8
(2) Suffering, *48 pp.*	1 3	1 5
(3) Loneliness, *72 pp.*	1 9	1 11
(4) Prayer, *64 pp.*	1 6	1 8
(5) Patience, *32 pp.*	9	11
(6) Peril, *64 pp.*	1 6	1 8
The Love of God		
The Graciousness of Uncertainty	9	11
The Message of Invincible Consolation	*each*	
Now is it Possible—		
The Sacrament of Saints	6	7
Oswald Chambers : His Life and Work	10 6	11 0
Seed Thoughts Calendar (*Perpetual*), 7th Series	2 6	2 8